boredom

peter toohey

boredom

a lively history

YALE UNIVERSITY PRESS | NEW HAVEN AND LONDON

For information about this and other Yale University Press publications, please contact:
U.S. Office: sales.press@yale.edu   www.yalebooks.com
Europe Office: sales@yaleup.co.uk   www.yalebooks.co.uk

Set in Arno Pro by IDSUK (DataConnection) Ltd
Printed in Great Britain by TJ International Ltd, Padstow, Cornwall

Library of Congress Cataloging-in-Publication Data

Toohey, Peter
  Boredom: a lively history/Peter Toohey.
    p. cm.
  ISBN 978–0–300–14110–8 (cl:alk. paper)
  1. Boredom—History. 2. Boredom. 3. Boredom in literature.
  I. Title.
  BF575.B67T66 2011
  152.4—dc22

                                                              2010041323

A catalogue record for this book is available from the British Library.
10 9 8 7 6 5 4 3 2 1

Contents

Illustrations

Preface

WHO CARES ABOUT boredom? It's trivial, and it's something that children suffer, isn't it? Yet boredom is one of the most unexpectedly common of all human emotions, and for that reason it shouldn't be ignored, or trivialized. It's part and parcel of ordinary life, something that Hanif Kureishi caught brilliantly in his novel about 1970s' London, *The Buddha of Suburbia*. Karin Amir, its half-Indian, half-Anglo hero is upbraided by his activist lover, Jamila:

'You're moving away from the real world.'

'What real world? There is no real world, is there?'

She said patiently, 'Yes, the world of ordinary people and the shit they have to deal with – unemployment, bad housing, boredom. Soon you won't understand anything about the essential stuff.'

Boredom may be a simple thing and it may be as basic as unemployment and bad housing, but it's a real emotion

1

that's been felt throughout history. As Jamila says, it's essential.

In more recent years, boredom has become the object of social and scientific analysis. One, slightly ironic, attempt at quantifying the incidence of boredom appeared in September 2009. According to an online survey conducted by the curiously titled commercial organization www.triviala.com the average Briton suffers from boredom for approximately six hours per week. That equates, over an average life span of 60.5 years, to more than two years of being bored – or, to put it differently, more than one twentieth of an average Briton's waking life is spent in a state of boredom. It's not possible to ascertain how reliable this statistic is, but a report in early 2009 by the London think tank the New Economics Foundation also made some startling claims for Britons' boredom. It asserted that UK citizens were the fourth most bored of the twenty-two nations in Europe. Britons were also reported as having the second lowest energy levels in Europe, which may help to explain their boredom: they simply lack the energy to amuse themselves. Nic Marks of the New Economics Foundation, writing without the hindsight of the bank collapses, reasoned that Britain was so bored and tired because 'the UK's long-hours culture and record levels of personal debt have squeezed out opportunities for individuals ... to ... pursue activities that would best promote personal and social well being'. It's not so different in the USA. One recent survey of approximately 400 secondary school students in the New England area reported that 9 per cent of these young people say that 'boredom is a real or serious problem in their lives, and

17 per cent note they are somewhat or completely dissatisfied with their lives'.

Rather than relying on what test subjects admit about their state of mind, other scientists have tried to find an objective scientific basis by which boredom can be measured. In 2009, neurologists at the University of Michigan, Ann Arbor, led by Daniel Weissman studied the interactions that occur between different areas of the brain when an individual falls victim to boredom. Several volunteers were placed inside a magnetic resonance imaging (MRI) room and subjected to tedious tasks for prolonged periods of time. They were asked, amongst other dreary things, to identify letters as they appeared on a screen. They had to do this for a full hour. Daniel Weissman and his team decided to direct their attention to those intervals when the concentration of the volunteers slipped. They hoped to be able to use the MRI data to see what happens inside brains when concentration attention fades and boredom takes over.

When the focus of the volunteers did begin to waver, Weissman and his collaborators noticed that areas of the brain closely related to self-control, vision and language processing seemed not to communicate with one another. They discovered that, as concentration ebbs, the intensity with which nerve centres link up also fades. 'This is equivalent to those regions disconnecting,' claimed Weissman, which seems to be linked with the feeling of boredom. What was particularly interesting about the experiment was that when the cranial crosstalk died down, particular regions of the cortex 'lit up'.

Daniel Weissman's experiment may have pointed towards boredom's headquarters (as it were), and provided a fascinating means by which the incidence of boredom can be tracked, but it does not explain what boredom is. So, what is it? My friend, the philosopher David Londey, once suggested to me that there might be no answer to this question. He suggested that boredom might not exist at all. Better, David speculated, to think of boredom as a grab bag of a term covering emotions such as frustration, surfeit, depression, disgust, indifference, apathy, and that feeling of being trapped or confined. When conditions like all of these are blurred together, he argued, people end up with a false emotion of boredom. Perhaps boredom is one of those old-fashioned terms, like consumption. It's a term that masks a constellation of independent disorders. David certainly had a point.

Before trying to address David Londey's worries, I'd like to look at what is normally meant by 'boredom'. Despite its ubiquitous usage there seem to be two main instances that the word describes. The *first* form of boredom is the result of predictable circumstances that are very hard to escape. Long speeches or long church services or long Christmas dinners are typical examples. This sort of boredom is characterized by lengthy duration, by its predictability, by its inescapability – by its confinement. And, when you feel like this, time seems to slow, to the point that you feel as though you stand outside of these experiences.

There are other characteristics. When an experience is repeated and repeated and repeated until the person undergoing it is utterly 'fed up', they will exclaim that they are bored.

Too much baklava can produce this sort of effect. There is usually a flavour of distaste or, more precisely, of disgust that comes about when one is *satiated* with a situation: so it is that terms such as nausea and biliousness are often used as other names for boredom. Boredom is an emotion usually associated with a nourished body: like satiety, it is not normally for the starving.

Boredom becomes worse when a situation seems valueless. A boring task, conversely, can become much more tolerable if it's aimed at what's thought to be a good end. Ironing and cooking, for example, can be pretty dull, but much less so when you do them for your children, rather than just for your solitary self. This relates to choice and to your little community. A boring task is always a boring task, but if you choose it (for some reasonable, communitarian end) its boringness is somehow mitigated.

There seems to be a stigma attached to experiencing this sort of 'simple' boredom. Perhaps this is because it is so often associated with children. I've often wondered if this stigma of childishness has given rise to the *second* form of boredom, occasionally termed 'complex' or 'existential'. (It was the German sociologist Martin Doehlemann who seems to have coined the expression 'existential boredom'.) This form of boredom is said to be able to infect a person's very existence and it may even be thought of as a philosophical sickness. It is no easy thing to characterize. Its complexity can take in many well-known conditions. These often go under such evocative names as melancholia, depression, ennui, *mal de vivre*, world-weariness, tristesse, *taedium vitae*, the Christian 'demon of noontide' or spiritual despair (named acedia or accidie), the French 'existentialist' nausea and despair, and many other comparable terms and conditions. It is the subject of most of the books written on boredom.

While this second form of boredom has caused the expenditure of a very considerable amount of black ink, very little has been devoted to the first form because it is dismissed as 'trivial'. But to my mind, existential boredom is a hotchpotch of a category, and one whose basis is more intellectual than experiential – it is a condition which seems to me to be more read about and discussed than actually experienced. This book will unapologetically give simple boredom an equal billing.

My late colleague David Londey was both wrong and right to suggest that boredom does not exist. To be fair to David, he didn't stick with his intuition, but he had made, as he always did, a very compelling and a very quirky point. Boredom does exist, but it exists as a much simpler, more normal and more useful emotion than most critics will allow. Existential boredom often seems more of an impressive intellectual formulation than an actual emotion. Simple boredom has a direct bearing on our ordinary emotional lives, keeping company (as I hope to show) with depression and anger while protecting us from their ravages.

But what boredom is and what it isn't is just the tip of the iceberg. Boredom lurks behind a surprising array of artworks, literature and films, as well as sociology, biology, psychology and philosophy. Neglecting to juxtapose these various manifestations of boredom, or privileging one over all others, risks losing some of the subtler shades of boredom and its remarkable history. Painters and novelists have an uncanny ability visually and descriptively to depict emotional states that puzzle or defy logic or reason. Through figuration and metaphor, art can grope beyond the limits of clarity and non-connotative language which quite rightly constrain the scientific disciplines, and tell us something about boredom without the need for a transparent linguistic term. But it also works the other way around: the science and theory behind boredom can re-illuminate certain very famous pieces of art and literature.

A confession. I've been bored for very large tracts of my life. Habitually bored. I suspect and I hope, but I cannot prove it, that boredom has done me no harm. That's beyond, perhaps, a lingering, but perfectly tolerable sense of uneasiness. But one thing I hope this book will illustrate is that boredom is, in the Darwinian sense, an adaptive emotion. Its purpose, that is, may be designed to help one flourish. In that sense, I can't help but feel that boredom has in some ways been a blessing. I do hope so. And I hope that I'll be able to demonstrate this in the pages that follow.

University of Calgary
14 August 2010

1

Putting boredom in its place

WHAT MAKES SOMETHING boring? Predictability, monotony and confinement are all key. Any situation that stays the same for too long can be boring. Road trips, gardening and – my own special bête noire – Easter religious services are all fertile sources of boredom. The three of them bedevilled my youth: I had to sit, trapped and wriggling, through the first and third and water the second again and again. A boring person will usually be predictable and repetitive as well, particularly in their speech. Like long-winded lecturers or relatives, the bore's droning, rheumy intonations don't seem to go anywhere, or at least not quickly enough. Their repetitive disquisitions confine you in a world of boring words. And time drags to a halt.

William Orpen's *A Bloomsbury Family* (1907) captures the excruciating sense of boredom caused by confinement. The family that is pictured is a well-known one: there is the father, the artist William Nicholson, with his wife, the painter Mabel Pryde, and (from left to right) his children, Nancy, who became the wife of the poet Robert Graves, Tony, who was killed in 1918 in the Great War, Ben, the well-known English abstract artist, and Christopher, an architect. But for all those connections, you can almost smell the boredom. William Nicholson presides over the table with the languorous disinterest of a school headmaster. The family either stares off into the middle distance or, like little Christopher, peers wide eyed

1 William Orpen, *A Bloomsbury Family*, 1907

and pleading to the viewer for help. Tony supports his drooping head with both elbows on the table (a dead giveaway for boredom), framed on either side by those of Ben and his father. In fact there's lots of framing in this picture – the overbearing pictures hanging on the walls, the rigid lines and corners used throughout the painting; and Orpen himself is even reflected in the convex mirror above the fireplace painting the family – this is the fourth wall, which only accentuates the sense of entrapment. Like Orpen, we get sucked into this boring, almost mesmerically dreary scene. You wouldn't want to be at that table for all the tea in China, or Bloomsbury.

Boredom breeds in stifling homes. Anton Chekhov, the great nineteenth-century Russian playwright and short-story author, mentions boredom more frequently than any other writer I have encountered (perhaps, as a physician, he was more interested than others in what goes on inside the human body) and his plays are packed with confining country homes. *Uncle Vanya* (1900), published not long before William Orpen painted his picture, is, like so many of Chekhov's plays and stories, constructed around the theme of boredom. The young, pretty and feckless Yeliena declares 'I'm dying of boredom . . . I don't know what to do'. She speaks for most of the characters in the play – evenings round the dinner table, with the same old faces, on country estates in the long Russian winters of the nineteenth century must have weighed very heavily on the privileged classes. Entrapment and sameness are the causes of this sort of boredom. Situations like these are trivial and are not normally long lasting, and escape eventually provides a remedy. Yeliena and her ageing husband, Professor Serebriakov, bolt from the country estate and head off to town.

This simple form of boredom is particularly associated with children: young Tony Nicholson was the most bored of a very bored family in William Orpen's painting, and Yeliena is not only the youngest person in *Uncle Vanya*, but childish to boot. Children have no shame when it comes to complaining of being bored. Adults, though never immune, are quick to deny they suffer from boredom – they're too grown up. Perhaps adults complain less because they feel that they should be able to stimulate themselves enough never to be bored – and many will brag that they never are bored. They are almost always lying.

I would defy any adult to drive along 'The Bore Track' and not suffer a severe bout of boredom. (It is not named for the obvious reason, unfortunately, but for the nearby gas fields, pipelines, and holes dug deep into the ground – bores – to which it provides access.) The scenery of the surrounding Strzelecki Desert is monotonous and repetitive, and it takes many hours to cross and escape the confines of the track. Imagine how the children would react if this were part of your holiday road trip.

You may be stifling a yawn just looking at this picture. It's easy to imagine how a luckless driver could snooze off to sleep, as they do occasionally on boring roads all the world over, and crash in broad daylight on a road like this. Yawning is as much a cousin of boredom as it is of tiredness. Andrew and Gordon Gallup, father and son psychologists at the State University of New York at Albany, have written that a person

2 'The Bore Track', Strzelecki Desert, South Australia

yawns to boost blood flow and to chill the brain, because the brain operates more efficiently when it's cool. 'According to our hypothesis,' they argue, 'rather than promoting sleep, yawning should antagonise sleep.' You'd need all the help you could get on the Bore Track.

The sort of boredom that is produced by the Bore Track and by the Nicholsons' dining room is sometimes termed 'situational' – a term also apparently first used by the German sociologist Martin Doehlemann. Another form of boredom derives its force from excess and repetition. Any experience that's repeated and repeated until you're fed up, until you're replete and stuffed, is termed by Lars Svendsen, that astute philosophical chronicler of boredom, 'boredom of surfeit'. It differs from the situational variety because the element of confinement is less pronounced.

As Christ prays in the Garden of Gethsemane on the evening before his final ordeal and crucifixion, could it be that the Apostles Peter, James and John suffer a biblical attack of the boredom of surfeit? The Good Book (Mark 14: 32–42) is inconclusive on this diagnosis but not so at least one of the many imagined versions of this scene. The beautiful rendition painted by the Renaissance artist Lo Spagna (d. 1528; his real name was Giovanni di Pietro) as *The Agony in the Garden* (1500–1505) makes this seem likely. Lo Spagna depicts the three Apostles with drooping heads and nodding off to sleep. Their heads rest on their forearms (one with his head on his hand, but the two Apostles flanking with their heads on their wrists). The position – which will come up later in this chapter – is a sign of boredom. The three Apostles should not be bored and sleepy. They ought to be full of attention and prayerful devotion. But they have had enough of their Easter service and this terrible garden. Their dereliction constitutes sin and it is expressed as boredom with the travails of their Saviour. The brilliant insight of Lo Spagna was to add this boredom to the usual depiction of the sleepy Apostles in Gethsemane.

Instances of this type of boredom in daily life, however, are usually much more prosaic. A friend of mine decided to listen to

3 Lo Spagna, *The Agony in the Garden*, 1500–1505.

Beethoven's piano sonata *The Hammerklavier* every evening for the best part of two months – which unsurprisingly became very boring indeed. She was not trapped by this experience, at least not in any obvious manner, for she could have chosen to stop listening at any point (although it is possible that there was an element of minor addiction involved). But her sonata surfeit did produce a strong feeling of disgust. She claimed that the sonata eventually made her want to vomit. Although that may be something of an exaggeration, disgust is an inherent aspect of the boredom brought on by predictability and repetition. William Ian Miller, in his evocatively titled book, *The Anatomy of Disgust*, notes with hesitation that 'boredom . . . is the name we give to a less intense form of disgust . . . Boredom stands in relation to disgust as annoyance does to anger.'

I'd like to pause over the connection between boredom and disgust, as it's a very important one for this book. The causal chain seems intuitive. Boredom is connected to surfeit; the experience of surfeit – of food or drink, most obviously – can induce nausea and even vomiting; and that leads to the disgust we feel at being sick. Consider the well-known expression 'I'm so fed up': it seems to imply that the speaker is surfeited even to the point of nausea or disgust. In my experience, people use the term as a means of describing acute boredom just as often as they do to indicate corporeal satiety.

Etymological digging into the word 'tedium', from the Latin *taedium*, also throws up an interesting connection. The Latin term, according to the Princeton Latinist Robert Kaster, encompasses weariness, boredom, and even disgust. Traces of this ancient complex of meaning can be found in the Latinate English phrase *taedium vitae*, which implies a weariness or boredom or disgust with life. This is the sort of world-weariness that Jean-Paul Sartre took as the subject for his novel *Nausea*. More of that later.

But there's more to the link between boredom and disgust than clever wordplay. In Guy de Maupassant's last novel, *Alien*

Hearts (1890), this intuitive connection between boredom and disgust is made wonderfully clear. Maupassant is speaking of his heroine, the bored coquette and salon hostess, Madame de Burne: 'And yet she was bored. How little she really enjoyed the society in which she had a secure position, enduring long evenings with stifled yawns and heavy eyelids ... [she was] attached just enough not to be too easily disgusted by what she had so lately enjoyed or admired ... she lived in a kind of lambent tedium.'

The psychologist Robert Plutchik offers a scientific psychological base for the bond between boredom and disgust. He maintains that emotions serve an adaptive role by helping creatures to cope with survival issues posed by their environment: disgust, for example, might keep animals and humans clear of noxious substances. Researchers at the London School of Hygiene and Tropical Medicine backed up this line of thought in 2004. Using a web-based questionnaire, they surveyed the responses of more than 40,000 subjects who were asked to decide which of paired photographs was the more disgusting: one photograph depicted a link to disease, the other did not. The majority of respondents found the disease-related image – of a towel with a brown stain on it, for example – more disgusting than that, say, of a towel with a blue stain on it. The researchers concluded that all animals avoid, and even fear, those things that carry disease, and that disgust is a form of evasive action designed 'to protect us against signs of disease' (*New Scientist*, 14 January 2004). Disgust, then, becomes an evolutionary response to 'dangerous items'.

Robert Plutchik, writing before this study, maintained that an emotion such as boredom emerges as a derivative or adaptation of this primary emotion of disgust. It serves, in his view, the same adaptive function, though in a milder or more inward-turning manner, as disgust. If disgust protects humans from infection, boredom may protect them from 'infectious' social situations: those that are confined, predictable, too samey for one's sanity. If all of this is true, then it might follow that boredom, like disgust, is good for you – I mean good for your health. Both emotions are evolved responses that protect from 'disease or harm'.

* * *

To worry over the distinction between situational boredom and boredom of surfeit is probably not worth the labour. In their way neither is chosen. Surfeit can be the result, for example, of mild addiction – say, to chocolate or to coffee. Addiction, whether mild or not, represents a type of confinement. In this book, therefore, I will treat these two forms of boredom more or less as a unit, termed *simple boredom*.

Simple boredom doesn't often make the news. One of its most recent and unusual appearances was in 2008, when the UK newspaper, the *Independent*, published a poll of public figures entitled 'The Boring List'. Victoria Beckham took the gong. Now, I've got no strong opinions on Victoria Beckham, but this doesn't seem to be a judgement on her personality: as a successful fashion designer and wife of the most famous footballer on the planet, being boring is not something I'd have associated with her. My occasional collaborator on this topic

4 Victoria Beckham

wonders if she topped the poll because she always seems to be photographed with the same rather blank expression. The Bore Track of all faces?

There are a series of codes – probably involuntary ones at that – for depicting boredom visually. The most arresting of these relates to the infinite, or at least a vista that is apparently endless. In artworks it's incorporated time and time again to represent and invoke a sense of boredom. Consider this strange painting by Arnold Böcklin, the underrated nineteenth-century German artist. Based on a legend from the first book of Homer's *Odyssey*, it offers a visualization of the

5 Arnold Böcklin's *Odysseus and Calypso*, 1883

exiled Odysseus trapped on Ogygia, the island of the goddess Calypso. Calypso has offered Odysseus a gift – immortality, a temporal version of the infinite – if he will stay as her lover. But he longs to go home. And in Böcklin's painting, shoulders hunched, spectre-like, he seems utterly bored. Neither Calypso's operatically sensuous body, nor that suggestive cave behind her, offers any promise of escape. Odysseus is bored stiff in this unchanging seaside paradise. Perhaps he can already see that an eternity of sex, even with an immortal goddess, would become pretty predictable.

Odysseus lurks at the back of the painting, staring across the sea towards Ithaca. But all Böcklin depicts is a blue-grey expanse, where you can't even distinguish sea from sky. This is the vast, unchanging infinite. Its effect is caught brilliantly in *Oblomov*, one of the very best books on boredom, written by the nineteenth-century Russian novelist Ivan Goncharov. Ilya Oblomov, the terminally bored hero, opines: 'The sea, for instance? Let it stay where it is! It merely makes you melancholy: looking at it you feel like crying. The heart quails at the sight of the boundless expanse of water, and the eyes grow tired of the endless monotony of the scene.' That seems to be just how Odysseus is feeling. There's nothing romantic in his posture, with his neck drooping and his dark, heroic body stooped. He's fenced in by an infinity of boring sameness within his gloomy, mythological Butlin's.

Infinity is of course temporal as well as spatial. Time has a very interesting relationship with boredom and its representations. We have all experienced the sluggishness of time when we have been confined in boring situations. According to one of the late Clement Freud's famous witticisms, 'if you resolve to give up smoking, drinking and loving you don't actually live longer, it just seems longer'. As Michael Raposa suggests in *Boredom and the Religious Imagination*, 'for the bored person, time seems to stand still'. In contrast, for a person totally absorbed in an enthralling task, the US psychologist and management professor Mihaly Csikszentmihalyi argues, time almost ceases. This is when you are 'in the flow', as Csikszentmihalyi puts it. Time in its normal course extends infinitely in either direction, but for those afflicted with boredom, it extends ever more slowly towards infinity.

It is no surprise that clocks become rich representational symbols of boredom and the tedium of time passing. A clock presides over the eerily still scene in a bizarre German painting by Carl Spitzweg, *The Cactus Lover* (1850). Its pendulum, frozen at the point from which it begins its swing to the

6 Carl Spitzweg, *Der Kaktusliebhaber* (*The Cactus Lover*), c. 1850

right, extends the moment infinitely. The whole scene points to the sort of confinement that causes boredom. The piles of apparently useless bound papers, the writings of the cactus lover perhaps, suggest that his reading public extends no further than his study. The cactus lover himself contemplates not the open window and what lies outside, but the friendly cactus plant, which strangely frames and echoes his posture (as does Böcklin's hunched-shouldered Odysseus). Coat and cactus are both ferruginous green. The only inkling of the exotic in this scene is the phallic plant itself, hinting mischievously at a world of vigour and manliness that is far removed. And cacti grow at an infinitesimal rate: more emphasis of the slowing or even of the cessation of time in this unchanging, interminable, boring room.

The infinite is probably the last thing on the minds of the couple portrayed in Walter Sickert's *Ennui* (1913). They seem desperate to escape the closed-in world of their lives. They are clearly bored: look at the woman's posture, with hunched shoulders and head cupped in her hand, and elbows resting on the drawers – mimicked by the man's right arm resting on the chair. His gaze is aimed into the middle distance, the woman's into the depths of the obscured painting above her head. Virginia Woolf commented on this painting in *Walter Sickert: A Conversation* (1934):

> . . . the old publican, with his glass on the table before him and a cigar gone cold at his lips, looking out of his shrewd little pig's eyes at the intolerable wastes of desolation in front of him? A fat woman lounges, her arm on a cheap yellow chest of drawers, behind him. It is all over with them,

7 Walter Sickert, *Ennui*, 1913

one feels. The accumulated weariness of innumerable days has discharged its burden on them.

Though exaggerated and wilfully inattentive, this passage does catch a little of the flavour of the picture and its yearning for an escape from ennui. It's hard not to agree with the phrase 'the accumulated weariness of innumerable days' (there's that sense of infinity again), even if Woolf's condescension of the 'little pig's eyes', the 'fat woman', and the 'cheap yellow chest of drawers' points to the snobbery of the author. Whoever these two victims of ennui are, they are both dreaming of escape, and the painting offers a few clues as to how they'd do it.

The bottle and a smoke are his remedy. Drugs and their comforting spirituous oblivion have always been one of the most efficient means for ridding a person of a bad dose of boredom. For the woman escape is whatever is in that obscured painting; one suspects it shows an exotic locale. Travel there would remedy the dismal boredom she is suffering – perhaps his, too. The portrait on the back wall offers another alternative: a teasing glimpse of the erotic.

These three remedies – drugged oblivion, travel and sex – are standard and clichéd cures for boredom, whether of the simple or the existential variety. Personal oblivion (the old man's answer) works, but at what cost? Oblivion brings with it a loss of the sense of self, through the eventual dimming of the memory: you're not you if you can't remember what you've done in your life. That loss is tantamount to death (a type of suicide). Pursuit of the erotic, the exotic or the new (the woman's answers – the last two might be termed 'getting away') are other options. But they never work. As fast as the new is experienced (whether exotic or erotic), it is liable to become boring. The new becomes a variant of the infinite. It recedes infinitely.

* * *

The pointlessness of 'getting away' as a remedy for boredom was brought back to me recently. Do you ever feel fed up on holiday? Look forward to getting home? In late August I received an alarming postcard. On one side it pictured an escapist beach scene. On the other side was written, simply, 'Had a wonderful holiday. Rained the whole time. Didn't have to take the children to the beach once. Got buckets of work done.' I showed it to a very hard working colleague (Stan, who is an academic, and who never takes holidays; he likes to brag 'work is the only holiday'). After he'd scanned the lines, he sighed, and said, 'I know how your friend feels. Holidays are so boring.'

If you really cannot escape boredom, then it seems to take on a different taste altogether. Boredom, when it persists and when it is related to something that matters emotionally, may seem to cripple. It's one thing to find a teacher or a road or a dinner party boring. Things like that can be finished with. It's something else suddenly to find your whole way of life or your heart's partner boring.

Boredom like this is perplexing. It so often has no apparent cause, can appear unexpectedly, and it can be hard or even impossible to cure. This sort of boredom, as I have explained earlier, is sometimes called 'existential' or 'spiritual', because it seems to affect a person's very existence. Writers and opinion makers usually believe that existential boredom is more important than simple boredom. They often suffer from it.

Sean Desmond Healy, in his *Boredom, Self, and Culture*, suggests that existential boredom – which he calls hyperboredom – entails 'the loss of a sense of personal meaning'. This can affect an individual in a 'spiritual' manner. It can cause in its victim an absence of desire. It can make a person believe that life is futile. It can even cause an individual to despair of the value of their own life and to give up their food. What's being discussed here is a philosophical sickness. In many ways it's a secular variant of the religious angst exhibited by Christians of many shades. What is God's plan? Where do I fit into God's plan and how do I live in it? What does God want me to do? Many God-fearing Christians will ask themselves questions like these. The more uncertain might respond to these perplexing questions with the same sort of passive, hopeless and depressive reactions that have been attributed to the sufferer of existential boredom. One of my Lutheran associates has explained these feeling to me like this:

'We Lutherans are in direct dealing with God and not with a lot of bureaucratic and priestly middlemen. But that also means that we Lutherans are responsible on God's behalf for doing good. And doing good is not a simple thing. Sometimes you simply don't know what good is. And that can be very worrying and depressing. But we are nevertheless responsible and don't expect the Holy Virgin to appear with a *dea ex machina* solution. Very simple, but not easy. We are as a result and by nature deeply worried and melancholic.'

These feelings are exacerbated if you don't believe in God. For such an individual the response to the question 'where do I fit in?' is often a brutal 'nowhere at all'. At this point you turn to the movies of Ingmar Bergman.

It will offend the thinkers, religious and atheist alike, if I pose the following suggestion: might not this existential form of boredom, this philosophical or even religious sickness, be best characterized as depression? Depression can mean anything from a mild but persistent sadness to a crippling psychological pain. And so too can this existential boredom. But if there is a difference between existential boredom and mild or clinical depression, might it not reside in the fact that this variant of boredom has become intellectualized? I don't want to press the similarities between existential boredom and depression too hard. David Londey's less precise evaluation – that this term may embrace a constellation of related disorders: frustration, surfeit, depression, disgust, indifference, apathy, and a feeling of being trapped – is the most convincing.

In her illuminating critical discussion of eighteenth- and nineteenth-century literary boredom, entitled *Boredom: The Literary History of a State of Mind*, Patricia Meyer Spacks astutely sums up what is generally understood by existential boredom, and its manifestation in our contemporary world:

Fictional (and poetic) evocations of boredom multiply exponentially in the twentieth century, partly for reasons implicit in the common understanding of modernism, which posits an isolated subject existing in a secularized, fragmented world marked by lost or precarious traditions: a paradigmatic situation for boredom. Boredom provides a convenient point of reference for the cultural and psychic condition of those deprived alike of meaningful work and of pleasure in idleness. At once trivialized and magnified, boredom in its early twentieth-century representations alludes to the emptiness implicit in a life lacking powerful community or effective tradition. Since 'everybody' feels it, it hardly distinguishes its sufferers. It can constitute a way of life, a fashion of speech, or both.

This form of boredom is not only believed to be widespread but is also understood to be a rather serious event. Existential boredom, to follow on from Spacks, can be described as a kind of 'emptiness' resulting from the sufferer's seeing him- or herself as isolated from others. Worse still, such individuals are living in a secularized world where religion no longer offers solace. They inhabit a fragmented and divided world where regional and even personal loyalties have been lost. This is a world from which tradition and community have disappeared. No wonder then that such modern individuals feel deprived of meaningful work and of meaningful idleness or leisure.

This alarming condition is often said to be the great characterizer of our age. Many people designate it as boredom, or existential boredom. And many others call it melancholy or even depression. The prize-winning critic Elizabeth Goodstein, for example, suggests in her *Experience without Qualities: Boredom and Modernity*, that the French poet Charles Baudelaire is a victim of existential boredom, while Jennifer Radden, in her influential and excellent compilation, *The Nature of Melancholy*, discusses the French poet within the long tradition of melancholy. The French critic Georges Minois also sees Baudelaire as a victim of depression: in France there is a tendency to ignore the notion of existential boredom and to term it melancholy. In fact the French display a remarkable enthusiasm for what they see as melancholy. I would estimate that during the year in which I first thought of writing this book, there were at least six books published in Paris with a variant of the word 'melancholy' in their title. In Anglo-Saxon circles 'boredom' would have been used instead.

Melancholy or existential boredom is a Gallic obsession. Such 'iconic' books as Gustave Flaubert's *Madame Bovary*, Jean-Paul Sartre's *Nausea* (the title intended by the author was *Melancholy*), or Albert Camus' *The Outsider* have this condition at their heart (these books will be discussed in later chapters). But it is not just the French who encourage this linguistic ambivalence. The Russians characterize the condition in a slightly different manner. John Anthony Cuddon's *Dictionary of Literary Terms and Literary Theory* (4th edn, 1998) highlights a genre called the 'superfluous man' (it sounds better in Russian: *lishni chelovek*). It was a very popular type in the nineteenth century and seems to have drawn its name from a short story by Ivan Turgenev entitled 'The Diary of a Superfluous Man' (1850). Here is J.A. Cuddon's summary of the genre:

It denotes an idealistic but inactive hero who is unaware of and sensitive to moral and social problems but who does not take action; in part because of personal weakness and lassitude, in part because of social and political restraints to freedom of action ... Turgenev tried to document and justify the existence of this type in Russian society, seeing him as a kind of a tragi-comic figure, a compound of Hamlet and Don Quixote, unable to reconcile the impulses of heart and head, given to over-much introspectiveness, intellectualizing, and indecision. Perhaps the most famous of all superfluous men is the endearing and totally ineffectual Oblomov in Goncharov's *Oblomov* (1859).

Being a superfluous man, being melancholic, suffering from existential boredom, being mildly depressive: all at different times can seem to be pretty much the same thing.

To illustrate the point, consider Oblomov, the poster boy of superfluity. One autumn evening the usual family members are gathered in the drawing room of their wealthy though thoroughly decrepit feudal estate, Oblomovka:

> The other inhabitants of the house and the usual visitors sat in the arm-chairs in the drawing-room in different positions, breathing hard. As a rule, deep silence reigned among them: they saw each other every day, and had long explored and exhausted all their intellectual treasures, and there was little news from the outside world. All was quiet; only the sound of the heavy, home-made boots of Oblomov's father, the muffled ticking of the clock in its case on the wall, and the snapping of the thread by the teeth or the hands of Pelageya Ignatyevna or Natasya Ivanovna broke the dead silence from time to time. Half an hour sometimes passed like that, unless of course someone yawned and muttered, as he made the sign of the cross over his mouth, 'Lord have mercy on us!' His neighbour yawned after him, then the next person, as though at a word of command, opened his mouth slowly, and so the infectious play of the air and

the lungs spread among them all, moving some of them to tears.

What is the matter with Oblomov's family? Are they melancholy? It certainly sounds like it. Are they depressed? Without a doubt. Are they bored? Absolutely. And could we call their boredom existential? I suppose that it is, for there is something almost spiritual in Oblomovka's surrender to sheer *existential* nothingness. The precise nature of existential boredom can therefore seem to be protean: depression, melancholy, superfluity, boredom, as well as a sense of frustration, surfeit, disgust, indifference, apathy, and a feeling of entrapment are all names of feelings to be associated with it. But, if existential boredom embraces such a multitude of conditions, whether it is a helpful concept at all for the understanding of human nature remains to be seen.

What, then, precisely links existential and simple boredom? To answer this requires a little more puzzling over their psychological status. Robert Plutchik, mentioned earlier in this chapter, was one of those who think of simple boredom as an emotion. Boredom, on this psychologist's understanding, is not quite a primary emotion such as, for example, happiness, sadness, fear, anger, surprise or disgust. Rather it has a derivative or secondary status, along with other emotions such as sympathy, embarrassment, shame, guilt, pride, jealousy, envy, gratitude, admiration, indignation or contempt. Emotions such as these are often termed social emotions. This means that they require other creatures for their acting out. Primary emotions seem to be, if not solitary things, at least emotions that have less need of social settings. You may fear an inanimate object: a falling tree, for example. But you are less likely to feel sympathy or envy for such an object.

How should boredom be thought of as an emotion? Emotions are not restricted to human beings. Many animals seem to feel primary emotions and many of them seem to feel the secondary or social emotions. The US neurologist Antonio Damasio suggests, in *Looking for Spinoza: Joy, Sorrow and the Feeling Brain*, that these two groups of emotions (the primary and the secondary) are not socially constructed but aim 'directly at life regulation by staving off dangers or helping an organism take advantage of an opportunity, or indirectly by facilitating social relations'. This is not to say that their enunciation may not be encouraged or hindered, or even shaped by their specific cultural circumstances. An ancient Greek was more prone to shame than to guilt, for example, while a modern Englishman is more prone to guilt than to shame. The social emotions of a chimp, for that matter, will not be those of a caterpillar.

Most emotions, whether primary or secondary, seem to be designed to assist humans and other creatures to navigate life successfully. They are adaptive, as neurologists such as Damasio term it. We may not admire some emotions – such as disgust or lust – but no emotion can ever be accused of being trivial or of being unnatural or of being a sickness or of being a weakness. Emotions have their own biological and adaptive roles and it is through the emotions that people learn how to adapt their behaviour fruitfully to the outside world and to come to protect themselves.

Simple boredom's connection to disgust has been noted by Robert Plutchik, William Ian Miller and Antonio Damasio. Boredom borrows its characteristics from this primary emotion. Antonio Damasio explains that disgust is 'a primary emotion that evolved in association with the automatic and beneficial rejection of toxic foods'. And boredom, according to William Miller, 'is the name we give to a less intense form of disgust'. The adaptive emotion of boredom has evolved therefore to facilitate social relations by encouraging the beneficial rejection of toxic social situations. Maybe this is how we should think of the common emotion of simple boredom. There's nothing childish about it. Nor should it be made somehow more respectable by refashioning it as a philosophical sickness. Boredom has its uses. It protects us in the same way that disgust does.

It is, however, very hard to imagine how existential boredom plays any of the adaptive roles that are often assigned to such emotions. It's a condition that entails a powerful and unrelieved sense of emptiness, isolation and revilement in which the individual feels a persistent lack of interest in, and difficulty with concentrating on, his current circumstances. It seems to afford its victims more heartache than protection. So, what are we dealing with here? Existential boredom is vastly too complex a condition to be termed, simply, an emotion. Antonio Damasio suggests that the 'sustaining of a given emotion over long periods of time' – depression, for example – should be thought of as a mood. Existential boredom might therefore better be nominated as such. Contrast simple boredom. It is no mood. It does not need to be sustained over long periods. Simple

boredom can be swift to appear, but, with the source of confinement or repetition suddenly removed, it's liable to vanish. That
existential boredom can persist like a very bad toothache points
again to the probability that what's being dealt with here is
simply something that's closer to a mood.

Or perhaps a 'feeling'? And what, for heaven's sake, is a
feeling? It is sometimes described as being the capacity to
sit back and contemplate your current emotional state. It
might well be defined as emotional self-reflectivity. Or, to put
it more simply, it is the capacity to recognize and to describe
the presence within oneself of an emotion.

Simple boredom is not a feeling because it has no need of
self-reflectivity for its existence. A small child, or indeed a
grown-up woman, can experience boredom without any
particular need to say what it is that they are feeling. I imagine
it is true that most humans quickly learn as children to recognize boredom, but most of them don't give very much thought
to its status. Nor do they begin to try to name it. At the very
most all they think about is escape. But existential boredom is
indeed the most self-reflectivity of conditions.

Whatever the actual nature of existential boredom, it does
not seem to share the emotional nature of simple boredom.
Perhaps the similarities go no deeper than a shared name. That
similarity may owe more to happenstance than to any profound
psychological similarities.

* * *

This consideration of the psychological nature of boredom is
getting closer to the aim of this chapter, to put boredom in its

proper place. There are telltale visual signs that give boredom away, in artworks as much as everyday life. It's an emotional state that's very hard to mask. It is possible to put boredom firmly in its place – visually.

Elbows that rest on flat surfaces such as tables or the arms of chairs, and forearms and hands that support heavy heads, are the commonest visual signals of boredom. If you are having a cup of tea with someone who has slowly sunk into this posture, then don't ask them what's wrong. Stop talking about yourself. You're boring them.

But if they are sitting on their own like this, then there could be something wrong. 'I discovered poor Maria sitting under a poplar,' Laurence Sterne tells us in his *Sentimental Journey* (1768). Maria was on her own and 'she was sitting with her elbow in her lap and her head leaning on one side within her hand'. What's the matter with young Maria? She's been jilted by a faithless lover. Maria's posture signifies melancholy. The Louvre's 'Mélancolie' exhibition of 2005 made this abundantly clear. Nearly all of the painted, sculpted and even photographed depictions of melancholy displayed heads on hands and elbows on flat surfaces, and the melancholic subjects were almost always alone. Melancholy and boredom may look alike. But boredom is a social emotion and it looks outward at a confining or monotonous situation. So it is with this Russian souvenir seller, with her head resting on the palm of her right hand, as bored as can be. Things will brighten up for her when she gets some customers. And although she appears to be alone, she is in Red Square, one of the most public of all places in Russia.

8 A woman sells souvenirs outside Red Square, Moscow, June 2008

Hands on hips are inverted hands on cheeks. The posture is one of the most obvious indicators of contempt and disgust – and disgust is intimately linked to being 'fed up', or bored. John Everett Millais' painting of Mariana (1851) from Shakespeare's play, *Measure for Measure,* is a good example. Millais was a Pre-Raphaelite artist with all of the romantic and nostalgic leanings that this designation implies. There's nothing very romantic about Mariana's posture: the posture that she adopts is a very unusual one. Lines from Alfred, Lord Tennyson's poem about Mariana, which were originally included with the painting, offer some help in understanding her emotion:

> She only said, 'My life is dreary.
>   He cometh not', she said;
> She said 'I am aweary aweary,
>   I would that I were dead!'

9 John Everett Millais, *Mariana in the Moated Grange*, 1851

Mariana lives a lonely, melancholy life. She has been rejected by her fiancé after her dowry was lost in a shipwreck. In Tennyson's poem, Mariana laments her lack of connection with all society. Mariana's hands-on-hips posture suggests not just backache (probably the result of her embroidery work), but also the distaste she feels for her dreary, boring and solitary existence without love.

Yawning is a giveaway indicator of boredom in real life or anywhere else. The bored Ilya Oblomov is a regular yawner. The author Alexander Zinoviev's enormous and bitter parody of a dreary 1960s' Soviet Russia under Nikita Khrushchev (the state is called Ibansk in this novel or Screwsville, as Clive James translates it) was entitled *The Yawning Heights* (1976). In visual art there are not many paintings of yawning, and not only because no one wants to see it depicted (it's too trivial), but yawning, because it exposes the interior of the mouth, is also far too personal. And ugly.

Yawns can express other emotions. Canines yawn to express unease or confusion, but they also yawn pleasure, as they don't know how to smile. When humans yawn, most often it's simply down to tiredness. It cools the brain, as the Gallups observed. No doubt Degas' ironing woman is fatigued if she has been sharing in the ironing that her partner is doing. But she isn't ironing and the bottle she clutches, though it presumably holds water to be used for damping the clothes to be ironed, could just as well hold wine and the prospect of escape from the drudgery. The position of her arms hints at the bored posture of the souvenir seller in Red Square, or of Millais' Mariana. Bored to tears – what else can the woman be? There's the repetitive task, confinement, yawning, stretching – all while her friend industriously ploughs on without even bothering to change her cooling iron. Byron neatly linked tiredness and boredom when he described boredom as 'that awful yawn which sleep cannot abate'.

Eyes that stare off into infinity in office meetings are some-times described as performing the 12-foot stare in a 10-foot

10 Edgar Degas, *Women Ironing, c.* 1884

room. It's also sometimes called the 'Antarctic stare', after the trance-like state that researchers in the Antarctic report occasionally experiencing. It's the result of too much or too little light, which disrupts the body's circadian rhythm and causes malfunctions in the normal distribution of hormones. But at business meetings, where staring into space is more commonly displayed, it is understood as a sign of boredom. The gaze is directed beyond the immediate and lost in an undefined distance.

Consider this beautiful young woman's unfocused gaze. It belongs to an unknown Athenian, Hegeso, whose well-known gravestone derives from the Ceramicus, the potters' area and burial ground near the ancient walls of Athens.

11 Funerary stele of Hegeso

Hegeso is seated on the right. A servant stands on the left holding what seems to be a jewel box. Look at Hegeso's lost gaze: it aims neither at what she holds in her right hand, nor at the box held by the servant, nor even at the servant herself. It peers off sadly into the indeterminate distance. If you did not know that Hegeso was dead, what would you take the expression to be? Boredom? Mourning and boredom, just like melancholy and boredom, are easily confused.

Necks that droop are characteristic of boredom as well as mourning. There's no need to make claims for the artistic value of William-Adolphe Bouguereau's *Le jour des morts* nor for his sentimental theme. It's enough to say that this painting and its ilk made Bouguereau both a very rich man and the butt of Degas' irony. But this tableau does provide a very neat illustration of the motif – one that we've already seen in Böcklin's hunched Odysseus – Bouguereau's drooping mourner. The woman's black-veiled head droops forward towards what is presumably her husband's grave, while her companion places a wreath. The drooping neck bespeaks mourning, perhaps because it is a very common sign of defeat. Think of athletes who have lost an important contest. Boredom comes when an unchanging situation has defeated our ability to keep interested. Boredom, melancholy, depression and mourning share common visual elements.

No bodies at all . . . This photograph of a canal scene, perhaps in Frinton in Essex (the photograph is labelled on the rear with 'Friton-England Plant'), is by Arthur Clegg Weston (1852–1913) a Victorian/Edwardian photographer. It is a very dreary commentary on work and industry. This is a landscape that should be busy. It's probably early morning, which

12 William-Adolphe Bouguereau, *Le jour des morts*, 1859

explains the empty scene, and the smoke coming from the chimneys of the workers' houses in the background suggests the coming bustle. So do the hoof-marked and worn towpath in the foreground and the big barge waiting to be loaded with all those casks. What makes the scene so boring? In part it's because of what's not there: people and animals and activity.

Remember the Bore Track? It too had that eerily empty quality. But Clegg Weston's version offers a special take on boredom. Frinton was a place where people laboured very hard at very menial jobs. The photograph creates a sense of bored anticipation. When will the tedium of the labour start?

Other elements in the scene compound the sense of boredom. There's too much sky, for one. Clegg Weston seems deliberately to want to emphasize its white-grey cloudiness, its opacity, its dreary endlessness. Nothing stands out. Even the silo building begins to fade into the mist. Nor is there any sun emerging from the clouds. The landscape is flat and, with the exception of the trees in the background and some down-trodden grass on the towpath, lacks even vegetable excitement.

13 Arthur Clegg Weston's photograph of Frinton, late nineteenth/early twentieth century

Clegg Weston's photograph highlights another important aspect of boredom. It is a social emotion, one played out mostly in situations where other people are present or should be present. Frinton and the Bore Track derive some of their dreariness from the noticeable absence of bodies. This scene, particularly as framed by Clegg Weston, is confining, unstimulating, somehow inescapable, and unchanging. These are precisely the sorts of feelings that might have been experienced by the labourers who actually inhabited the world of this strangely piercing photograph.

These images, drawn from a variety of historical periods and genres, suggest that there is a timelessness to the appearance of simple boredom. When I say this, however, I can see my learned old friend, David Konstan, the historian of the emotions from Brown University and NYU, shaking his ever smiling head. Peter, he'd say, don't you know that Charles Darwin failed to show this as far back as 1872 with the photographs in his book, *The Expression of the Emotions in Man and Animals*? Emotions, David would say, are *cognitive* events. This means that an emotion for a human entails not just a *reaction* (say, of disgust at a piece of mouldering green tofu), but at the very same time an *evaluation* (so I will examine the offensive tofu to ascertain its edibility). David and many other cognitivists believe that the evaluative element of emotion is conditioned by the habits of particular societies, historical periods, languages, and even particular genders. Thus, he might patiently explain, in some societies disgust might be thought of as a deliberative emotion, because it makes you evaluate toxins. The visual reaction to gone-off food in such a society might be a thoughtful and furrowed brow. In other societies, given to more performative emotional display, rotten tofu might cause a person to throw up their hands in horror and to walk away quickly. These are markedly different visual displays of disgust.

David's is a very powerful argument. I will return to it later in the book. For now let me say that in my opinion the cross-cultural and historical evidence that I have looked at suggest, in the case of boredom, that there are a small number of basic visual cues to its presence. The most powerful are yawning and the head cupped in the hand, but the others that I have illustrated are comparably widespread. These seem to be displayed in most societies.

* * *

So, it is beginning to become clear what simple boredom looks like. A definition of boredom might go something like this: it is an emotion which produces feelings of being constrained or confined by some unavoidable and distastefully predictable circumstance and, as a result, a feeling of being distanced from one's surroundings and the normal flow of time. But that is very cumbersome. One of the tests for a good definition is that it's easy to remember. Let's try again: Boredom is a social emotion of mild disgust produced by a temporarily unavoidable and predictable circumstance.

But even that's not the whole story. What boredom actually *is* may be traced to a lack of the neurotransmitter dopamine. Dopamine is the reward system of the brain. This brain chemical has been linked to such emotions as joy and excitement. It triggers a response in human brains that in a sense *is* these emotions. Dopamine depletion would make both of these much harder to experience. And it has been shown to lie at the heart of both the trance-like Antarctic stare and the hyper-activity of children with Attention Deficit Hyperactivity Disorder (ADHD). These children find periods of inactivity excessively boring because a lower level of dopamine affects their sense of time; for them, unoccupied minutes pass more slowly, so they feel bored much more quickly than others with normal levels. Katya Rubia of the Institute of Psychiatry at King's College, London, reported that 'novelty-seeking and risk-taking' is the way that these children 'self-medicate' and boost their dopamine levels, thus normalizing their time perception and curing their boredom. Ritalin is prescribed for the same reason.

It has been argued that boredom-prone individuals may have a naturally lower level of dopamine. This may mean that they require a heightened sense of novelty to stimulate their brains – to get the dopamine flowing, in other words. And it has also been argued by neurologists that in such individuals 'the long variants (7 repeat or more) of the dopamine receptor D4 (DRD4) cause dopamine to be consumed more quickly by the brain'. Individuals with this variant seem to display a thrill-seeking, adventurous personality, perhaps to make up for their lower than average dopamine levels. The Antarctic stare also shows how individuals, not necessarily affected by naturally low dopamine levels, can come to suffer dopamine depletion and the consequent boredom-like symptoms. Environment, not just genes, can cause boredom.

But there do seem to be some individuals for whom boredom is more of a problem than it is for others, individuals who could be described as prone to boredom. For them the emotion can represent a chronic problem – and when it does become chronic, boredom seems to be accompanied by a variety of other problems, many of which can be related to risk-taking, such as drugs, drinking, a hot temper and promiscuity. Boredom in itself is a beneficent emotion, but not perhaps when it becomes chronic. It's this baleful chronicity that will be the theme of my next chapter.

2

Chronic boredom and the company it keeps

THE STATEMENTS TO follow can be answered using a 7-point scale – from '1' (highly disagree), to '4' (neutral), to '7' (highly agree).

1. It is easy for me to concentrate on my activities.
2. Frequently when I am working I find myself worrying about other things.
3. Time always seems to be passing slowly.
4. I often find myself at 'loose ends', not knowing what to do.
5. I am often trapped in situations where I have to do meaningless things.
6. Having to look at someone's home movies or travel slides bores me tremendously.
7. I have projects in mind all the time, things to do.
8. I find it easy to entertain myself.
9. Many things I have to do are repetitive and monotonous.
10. It takes more stimulation to get me going than most people.

11. I get a kick out of most things I do.

12. I am seldom excited about my work.

13. In any situation I can usually find something to do or see to keep me interested.

14. Much of the time I just sit around doing nothing.

15. I am good at waiting patiently.

16. I often find myself with nothing to do – time on my hands.

17. In situations where I have to wait, such as a line or a queue, I get very restless.

18. I often wake up with a new idea.

19. It would be very hard for me to find a job that is exciting enough.

20. I would like more challenging things to do in life.

21. I feel that I am working below my abilities most of the time.

22. Many people would say that I am a creative or imaginative person.

23. I have so many interests, I don't have time to do everything.

24. Among my friends, I am the one who keeps doing something the longest.

25. Unless I am doing something exciting, even dangerous, I feel half-dead and dull.

26. It takes a lot of change and variety to keep me really happy.

27. It seems that the same things are on television or the movies all the time; it's getting old.

28. When I was young, I was often in monotonous and tiresome situations.

The test is called the Boredom Proneness Scale (BPS). It was devised in 1986 by the now retired psychologist Norman D.

Sundberg of the University of Oregon and his then student Richard F. Farmer. It judges an individual's capacity to become easily bored. To find out your own proneness to boredom, give yourself a score for each of the questions on a scale of 1 to 7 and add up the total. The average range for scores is 81–117, while the average itself is 99. If you scored high on this test, above 117, then you become bored very easily indeed. But if you scored lower than 99 or even below 81, then your boredom threshold is very high. You don't bore easily at all.

This test is said to allow psychologists to separate individuals who suffer transient boredom from those who suffer chronic boredom. Transient boredom is something that all people feel from time to time. It's reasonable to experience this sort of boredom while stuck in a queue or in one of my lectures, for example, and it passes quickly. But chronic boredom is another matter altogether. It does not pass quickly. Psychologists agree that it's entirely unreasonable to experience the sort of chronic boredom that makes Goncharov's Ilya Oblomov behave so indolently upon waking:

> As soon as he had got up in the morning and had taken his breakfast, he lay down at once on the sofa, propped his head on his hand and plunged into thought without sparing himself till at last his head grew weary from the hard work and his conscience told him that he had done enough for the common welfare. Only then did he permit himself to rest from his labours and change his thoughtful pose for another less stern and business-like and a more comfortable one for languorous day-dreaming.

Oblomov's passivity may seem humorous and harmless, but many psychologists are very concerned about people like him. The science writer Anna Gosline (in her 2007 article 'Bored?') reports that 'people who are often [chronically] bored are at greater risk of developing anxiety, depression, and drug or alcohol addiction, displaying anger, aggressive behaviour, and lack of interpersonal skills, and performing poorly at work and at school'. Such conclusions are backed up by a number of studies. In 2003, for example, a report was published on the website of the National Center on Addiction and Substance Abuse (CASA) at Columbia University in the USA which maintained that more than half (52 per cent) of teens are in danger of slipping into substance abuse if they fall prey to any one of three risk factors: feeling stress, being frequently bored, or having too much spending money. Two or more can be 'catastrophic', Joseph Califano Jr, the chairman of the Center, is quoted as saying. The poll was based on 1,987 teenagers aged between 12 and 17. Califano believes that parents should see boredom as a 'red flag'.

So if that's the case, chronic boredom is potentially a dangerous emotion. The converse is also true. People who suffer only transient boredom, and who ranked low on the BPS scale, were found to perform better in a wide variety of aspects of their lives, including career, education and personal autonomy. The BPS, as a result, has been applied in work-places and educational forums. It is believed to enable the tester to spot those who are liable, because of their chronic boredom, to cast a pall over the workplace, or to explain the reasons why some children are inattentive and disruptive and perform poorly at their lessons. Some psychologists use the BPS to predict whether a patient may be prone to certain more dangerous states, such as those that Anna Gosline mentions.

But before we all start worrying over our own scores (and, perhaps more so, over those of peculiar work colleagues or unruly children), it's worth reflecting on the test itself. Not only is the BPS comprised of relatively few, and very obvious, questions; it's also been suggested that you need to add or subtract 10 per cent to or from your score according to your current mood. Feeling cheerful means you'll score as less boredom prone, whereas a gloomy frame of mind will increase your tally. But the usefulness of the BPS as a predictor of pathological behaviour picks up a theme that will be seen often in this book: the link between boredom and an agitated or angry disposition. The connection was made by the German psychiatrist Otto Fenichel (and by Theodor Lipps before him). Fenichel, in a 1951 volume entitled *Organization and Pathological Thought*, argued that chronic boredom transformed into not just pathological behaviour, but something which he termed pathological boredom. This was due to the repression of normal human drives and desires. Boredom for Fenichel was a means by which restlessness, excitement and even anger could be controlled and disguised. So he contends of one of his clients that 'the boredom which the patient experienced denied his excitation'. This sort of repression on the part of boredom, he believed, was pathological because it stopped the normal expression of these emotions and hence encouraged neurosis.

Chronic boredom can be understood by likening it to anger. Most people suffer occasional feelings of anger – transient bursts of frustration or rage, it could be said. But everyone has known people who seem to be persistently angry. Whether it's politics, the weather or their boss, they remain in a permanent state of incandescence. I've known dogs like this too: the slightest provocation seems to make them want to bite and bark. Occasional or transient anger usually has an easily identifiable, easily forgivable origin. But what is it with these permanently angry types? Their chronic anger seems to be 'without cause' – or at least to have a cause so obscure that a decently trained psychiatrist would have trouble getting to the bottom of it. Thus it is with boredom. Some individuals seem to get bored more easily and more often than others.

The actual nature of the chronic boredom suffered by these individuals doesn't seem to be any different from transient boredom. It's important to recognize this. The difference between chronic boredom and transient boredom is strictly one of duration. It's usually said that some sufferers have a metabolic proneness to chronic boredom; that's just another way of alluding to the lower-than-normal dopamine levels, the neurochemical basis that exacerbates one's proneness to becoming bored.

Like ADHD children, the chronically bored seem to be more liable to self-medicate through sensation-seeking behaviour. Alcohol, as we saw in Sickert's *Ennui*, is a long-standing solution to boredom. The German neurologist G.W. Wiesbeck in a 1995 study compared fifteen alcoholic men with a family history of alcoholism, and fifteen alcoholics without a family history of alcoholism, with fifteen healthy men from a disease-free background. The scientists artificially stimulated the production of dopamine in each of the groups, but found that only the first two groups (the alcoholics with and without a family history of the disease) had unusually large amounts of dopamine activity subsequent to the experiment. Unable to modulate their dopamine levels, which swung under stimulation with apomorphine from lower than normal to a very high level, these groups therefore seem to have a greater propensity to risk-taking behaviour, in this case consuming too much alcohol. (The need was greatest in the first group, those with a family history of drinking.) Dangerous behaviour is linked to a physiological need to overcompensate for lower than normal levels of dopamine activity – in other words, something close to being bored.

Even more far reaching results were achieved by two teams of researchers, one at Vanderbilt University in Nashville, the other at the Albert Einstein College of Medicine in New York City. They looked at the connection between dopamine and personalities who were drawn to a variety of risk-taking and sensation-seeking behaviours. Led by Professor David Zald from Vanderbilt University, the researchers studied thirty-four men and women and, by examining factors such as decision-making speed, spontaneity, and adherence to rules, ranked the individuals on a 'novelty-seeking' scale. Utilizing positron emission tomography (the PET scan) these neurologists charted the subjects' brains, and looked particularly at their dopamine-regulating receptors. Individuals who had been classed as novelty-seekers were found to have fewer dopamine receptors. Their brains are less efficient at modulating levels of dopamine, so during dangerous or thrilling activities, individuals with fewer delimiting dopamine receptors seem to gain the greatest stimulation. No wonder they then keep doing whatever it is that gives them this incredible stimulation. Parachuting, driving too fast, spending too much, engaging in illicit sexual behaviour, as well as taking drugs, are all drawn into this dopamine-driven web.

Flirting with the illegal, even the very act of drug taking, produces heightened dopamine activity in the brain (as does the drug itself). This dissolute crew of dope fiends look so euphorically vacant that boredom would not even be a

14 Opium smokers in the East End of London, 1874

possibility – thanks to the rampant activity of the dopamine. But does the posture of the man at the top-centre of the picture hint at the boredom that the group are endeavouring to escape – and which will inevitably return? What other recourse will there be but to seek more sensation?

Thus it is as Anna Gosline reports in her 2007 article 'Bored to Death': the chronically bored 'are at higher risk for depression, anxiety, drug addiction, alcoholism, compulsive gambling, eating disorders, hostility, anger, poor social skills, bad grades, and low work performance'. But which comes first? Does chronic boredom cause pathological behaviours? Or is it itself a pathological behaviour (albeit a muted one) produced by lowered levels of dopamine activity? The research seems to suggest that chronic boredom is one of the symptoms of this chemical imbalance, along with risk-taking and sensation seeking. It is not a causative agent. It is incorrect to link chronic boredom and pathological behaviour in a cause and effect manner. Rather, a dopamine imbalance causes chronic boredom as well as potentially a host of more serious complaints. Boredom cannot get the blame here. It causes nothing.

James M. Cain's famous novel, *The Postman Always Rings Twice* (1934), is one of the best exemplars of this dangerous blend of risk-taking, sensation seeking and chronic boredom. William Marling, the author of *The American Roman Noir* (1998), suggests that the plot of *The Postman* may derive from one of the most sensational news stories of 1927 and 1928, the trial and execution of 'Tyger Woman', a 31-year-old blonde mother named Ruth Snyder, and her lover, the corset salesman Judd Gray, for the murder of her husband Albert.

Ruth Snyder, a sensation seeker and a risk taker if ever there was one, persuaded her lover to assist her in attempting to murder Albert with a panoply of weapons: alcohol, chloroform, garrotte wire, followed by a belt to the head with a sash weight. It was the chloroform that killed him. Raised dopamine activity, certainly, but I don't see much chronic boredom in the sad tale of these two unfortunate psychopaths. James M. Cain seems to have thought differently. He made chronic boredom and a longing to escape it the motivator for his unfaithful heroine, Cora.

In Cain's novel the story is told by Frank Chambers, an easily bored drifter. Frank is a product of the Great Depression. His preference for the road and for a life of bit jobs is born out of an era of serious – and bored – unemployment. One day Frank stops at a petrol station cum sandwich joint for a meal, and winds up working there. The Twin Oaks Tavern (which has no liquor licence) is run by the hellcat Cora and her much older husband, Nick Papadakis, 'The Greek'. She'd married Nick to escape her chronically boring life working in a Los Angeles hash house, but look where she wound up. The young Frank and Cora are drawn together at once and they begin a sensation-filled affair: 'I took her in my arms,' Frank tells us, 'and mashed my mouth against hers . . .' "Bite me!" I bit her.' Sick of her loveless life in the dreary diner Cora decides to take a big risk: killing Nick the Greek. She and Frank can then start a new, boredom-free life in the rejuvenated gas station. Coshing Nick in the bathtub while he sings 'Mother Machree' fails to do the job. 'The Greek' recovers, but his amnesia protects the lovers. After Frank and Cora get Nick drunk, cosh him again and kill him, they disguise the murder as a car crash. The police are suspicious and the cagey prosecutor Sackett schemes to split the lovers' loyalty by trying Cora alone. The ploy fails. Cora plea-bargains and is given a suspended sentence.

It's at this point that the storyline goes haywire. Sensing improbability, Cain tries to cover things up with an increasingly labyrinthine plot. The wildly escalating drama is anything but boring. Frank and Cora, against all expectation, are reunited, and everything seems to be going well at the gas station. But now it is Frank who is getting bored with this conformity and, when Cora returns to Iowa for her mother's funeral, he begins an affair with the puma trainer Madge Allen. But Cora returns pregnant and the couple are reunited again. Too bad that, soon after, Cora dies coincidentally in a second car crash. Frank, as his narrative explains, was convicted of responsibility for this second accident and has completed this novel just before his own execution. It's a great book. Norman Mailer thought *The Postman* was one of the ten best ever American novels.

Frank and Cora are chronically bored sensation seekers who break the law – and Cain isn't the least interested in which caused which. Not all fiction is as percipient as *The Postman*. It seems logical, at an intuitive level, to view boredom as the cause of a variety of villainy, rather than as just a companion. Victor Maskell, the predatory, frosty and utterly engaging central character in John Banville's ravishing 1997 novel, *The Untouchable*, is such a villain. During the 1930s, while still a young man at Cambridge, Maskell had become an agent for the Soviet Union. He is based on the infamous Anthony Blunt, Surveyor of the Queen's Pictures, who was unmasked in 1979 as having spied for the Soviets. *The Untouchable* charts Maskell's recollections about his own past and the motives for his betrayal. Why would the aristocrat Victor Maskell have turned his back on his upper-class upbringing as a bishop's son and become, of all things, a communist spy? One of the motives adduced by Banville is the fear, on Maskell's part, of chronic boredom. Spying was his self-medication. Maskell admits as much to the reader:

> 'Why did you do it' Miss Vandeleur said . . .
> 'Why,' I said. 'Oh, cowboys and Indians, my dear; cowboys and Indians.' The need for amusement, the fear of boredom: was the whole thing much more than that, really, despite all the grand theorising?

If Maskell had done the BPS and met Question 25 ('Unless I am doing something exciting, even dangerous, I feel half-dead and dull') he'd have answered with a bold 7.

But it's not really credible. Banville sometimes has Maskell dig deeper, beyond trite cause and effect:

> Have I lived at all? Sometimes the chill thought strikes me that the risks I took, the dangers I exposed myself to . . . were only a substitute for some more simple, much more authentic form of living that was beyond me.

If it's not driving the Victor Maskells into villainy, then chronic boredom seems to represent a deep psychological malaise that is caused by the even deeper inequities of the modern world. Maskell has given himself up to the 'grand theorising' here. Whether he claims his acts of betrayal were because he wanted to escape his boring life, or because he could not achieve his escape, perhaps he, or Banville, should not appeal to boredom and should admit to responsibility.

Boredom doesn't *cause* anything. Rather, boredom, or more particularly chronic boredom, can accompany or even be caused by more fundamental conditions such as personality or personal physiology. So, extroverts are more prone to boredom than introverts – and it seems to be their extroversion that drives their boredom, not the other way around. A number of studies have suggested that those who rely more on external than internal stimulation often perform worse on repetitive and predictable tasks: boring tasks, that is to say. This is usually attributed to their needing greater stimulus from their environment and their inability to generate their own stimulation. It's been suggested as well that men rely more on external stimulation than do women. If this is turned off then they'll readily complain of boredom. People who lack self-awareness are also said to be more prone to boredom. This was the conclusion of a 1998 study by Hope Seib and Stephen Vodanovich. In their examination of 308 Florida college students, those who ranked high in self-awareness (the ability to 'mood label') scored lower on the BPS. It's also been argued that people who have trouble describing their feelings or who have an impoverished emotional or fantasy life are more prone to boredom too.

Boredom is associated with some brain injuries. Investigations into traumatic brain injury (TBI) have opened up an interesting line of speculation on the nature of the body chemistry behind boredom. Anna Gosline (in 'Bored to Death') points out that TBI victims apparently suffer more from chronic boredom than might have been expected. James Danckert, a neuroscientist from the University of Waterloo in Ontario, has observed that people with TBI often begin to undertake more dangerous activities, such as drug taking or parachuting, than they did before their trauma. He speculates, according to Gosline, that 'the massive influx of endorphins or pain medication necessary for recovery from a brain injury may have literally raised these patients' threshold for psychological pleasure and reward'. Time will tell whether this speculative line will hold water. But there is no necessary cause and effect here, regarding boredom, just a fascinating association.

* * *

Chronic boredom and anger enjoy a very special, even symbiotic companionship. This alarming blend is strikingly encapsulated in Edgar Degas' imposing, fiery painting, *La Coiffure* (1892–1895). It offers a fascinating example of how art can intuitively represent the arresting mix of boredom and anger. A very large and dominating canvas, it hangs in one of the first halls in the National Gallery in London. Its commanding size is intensified by its striking colour. It's nearly all red: the background wall, the curtain, the dress of the woman whose hair is being combed, her hair, and that of the servant who is doing the combing.

The pursed lips of the woman who is having her hair combed point to the painfulness of the combing and her anger

15 Edgar Degas, *La Coiffure (Combing the Hair)*, 1892–1895

at having to put up with such a mauling. The coarse texture of the blood red painting also lends it a fire-like, furious tenor. But there is a sense of boredom here too. This young woman is trapped in a painful, repetitive situation. And notice her right hand that is held up to the head: rather than merely aiming to assuage the pain, the position of her arm is strongly evocative of boredom's body language, as we saw in the previous chapter. The social emotion seems to have infected the maid too, who looks politely resigned or, rather, bored. The curtain closes off the women's lives from the amusements of the wider world, adding to the sense of confinement.

Psychological enquiries empirically validate this intuitive understanding. It was the Freudians and the psychoanalysts who first got the ball rolling. Otto Fenichel and a number of other analysts believed that boredom is the outcome of anger, rather than the other way round. Because 'nice people don't get angry', they reasoned that individuals transform the anger and hostility, that would otherwise be turned against themselves, into boredom. It is an attempt at self-protection. People use boredom as an 'anger equivalent', and as a means for disguising their angry feelings both from themselves and from others.

Stephen Vodanovich, who has devoted a large share of his working career as a psychologist to investigating boredom, makes the link between it and anger in a much more common-sense way. Sundberg and Farmer's Boredom Proneness Scale, according to the research of Vodanovich and his colleague Deborah Rupp, makes it clear that 'individuals with the tendency to experience boredom [subject to chronic boredom, that is to say] may be at an increased risk for feelings of inner anger, as well as having a lowered ability to restrain their anger'. Those people who scored highly on his BPS 'had significantly greater levels of self-reported anger and aggression'. This connection was borne out by a careful study entitled 'Boredom proneness in anger and aggression: effects of impulsiveness and sensation seeking' by Eric Dahlen and his team from the University of Southern Mississippi. They aimed to find a solid statistical basis for the connection between boredom and anger. Two hundred and twenty-four university student volunteers completed a battery of tests designed to rate their boredom proneness, impulsiveness, sensation seeking, anger expression and aggression. Dahlen and his team conclude that 'boredom due to a lack of external stimulation predicted one's propensity to experience anger, maladaptive anger expression, aggression, and deficits in anger control'. Their findings demonstrate that boredom proneness has more pervasive effects on aggression than do any of the other variables.

If you live near the Rocky Mountains, as I do, there's a condition that vacationers often speak of that blends boredom with anger: cabin fever. It offers a vivid illustration of Vodanovich's and Dahlen's themes. A truly flamboyant and insightful representation of cabin fever and its association between chronic boredom and anger can be found in Stephen King's popular novel *The Shining* (1977). If you haven't read the book, then you are sure to have seen Stanley Kubrick's famous filmed version (1980). Although they do differ on quite a number of points, both plots are driven by chronic boredom that feeds off and amplifies violent anger.

Jack Torrance (played in Stanley Kubrick's version by Jack Nicholson) is a former teacher dismissed from his job for assaulting one of his students. Mercurial, selfish and now unemployed, his chronic boredom has an unexpectedly catastrophic effect. Having applied for a winter job as a caretaker at the Overlook Hotel in the Colorado Rockies, he's keen to sort out his life after his drink-addled fiery temper cost him that teaching position. Mr Ullman, the hotel manager, warns Jack that he and his family will be snowbound through most of the winter. Their chances of contracting cabin fever – the upshot of unrelieved boredom – are high. Mr Ullman explains the condition to Jack:

> 'It's a . . . claustrophobic reaction that can occur when people are shut in together over long periods of time. The feeling of claustrophobia is externalized as a dislike for the people you happen to be shut in with. In extreme cases it can result in hallucinations and violence – murder has been done over such minor things as a burned meal or an argument about whose turn it is to do the dishes.'

Jack Torrance knows better than Mr Ullman. Boredom is the domain of the uneducated. Only the kind of man with no interests would go downhill so quickly, as Jack explains:

> 'there's nothing to do but watch TV . . . So he drinks himself to sleep and wakes up with a hangover. He gets edgy . . . Finally . . . boom, boom, boom.'

Besides, Jack has his play to finish writing. The job is an opportunity to set his life in order, to keep off the grog, and to find his way out of 'that interesting intellectual Gobi known as writer's block'. Jack blames his life-problems for this scribal stall, but it seems more likely to have been the product of the boring years spent teaching at Stovington where he had felt 'stifled, buried alive'. Jack ignores Mr Ullman's warning and accepts the job. He would have scored very badly on the Boredom Proneness Scale. It's a real shame that Mr Ullman didn't administer the test to all of his job applicants before he hired them.

Things don't work out. The Overlook is of course haunted, and Jack succumbs lethally to the influence of its supernatural inhabitants. But both King and Kubrick emphasize the corrosive power of simple boredom, too. Wendy, Jack's wife, describes his increasing tetchiness as he starts to try and write his play: 'Long pauses at the typewriter, more balls of paper in the wastebasket . . . He got irritated over little things . . . Increased profanity.' In the first of the film's scenes in which Jack is attempting to write, Kubrick shows him bouncing a ball against the wall of the hotel's Colorado Lounge, a characteristically bored action which is laced with aggression. The content of Jack's manuscript appears later in the film: hundreds of pages comprised of a single repeated sentence, 'All work and no play make Jack a dull boy'. He is chronically bored, though terrifyingly far from 'dull'.

Chronic boredom keeps company with another dissolute crowd: the angry, the risk takers, the sensation seekers, the substance abusers. Paranoia, another member of the company that chronic boredom frequents, may help to provide a more solid idea of how common boredom is. The research psychologist Mitchell J. von Gemmingen has made a fascinating and convincing case for the association of the two. Von Gemmingen's research suggests that boredom proneness may be seen as a 'springboard' towards feelings of paranoia, especially for males. He infers from his statistical data that 'boredom prone people share characteristics with paranoid individuals such as harbouring resentment towards others and perceiving others as both threatening and as potential enemies feigning friendship'. So, people who show mild levels of paranoia are more prone to experience chronic boredom.

Now, reliable statistics on the frequency of chronic boredom in normal populations are hard to come by, but there are indications of the rates of paranoia, which might provide a basis for speculation. Daniel and Jason Freeman, in their entertaining book, *Paranoia: The 21st-Century Fear*, report an interesting experiment carried out in London in the summer of 2006. One hundred men and one hundred women, aged 18–77 and from various socio-economic backgrounds, were made to wear virtual-reality headsets. They watched a simulation of a four-minute ride on a London Underground train. The normal sights and sounds of the tube ride were replicated. The train was even crowded with computer-generated characters (avatars). 'These avatars,' the Freemans explain, 'were programmed to be absolutely neutral – neither friendly nor threatening. Some of the avatars would glance at the participant, though only after the participant had been looking at them for some time. One avatar would smile if the participant gazed at them.' Most participants in the Freemans' experiment reported that the avatar passengers behaved in a neutral manner. But only just 'most'. Apparently 45 per cent of the participants had at least one paranoid thought during their experience. For them the avatars were registered as anything from seducers to pickpockets.

The Freemans believe that paranoia is very common in modern societies. They point out elsewhere in their book that 'when a research team contacted 500 Londoners seven months after the attacks on the underground of July 7, 2005, they found that not only a significant proportion were still fearful of travelling on the tube, but that almost 25 per cent had a more negative view of the world since the bombings.' While this fearfulness may have some justification, the Freemans view it as excessive and therefore as reflecting a real paranoia.

There's nothing absolutely conclusive here. But it does seem to suggest that a significant number of normal individuals regularly entertain *some* paranoid feeling. In times of stress, which they believe Londoners are certainly living through at this moment, one in four normal people would seem to be *mildly* paranoid.

What does this say of the frequency of chronic boredom? Nothing definitely. But if there is an association between paranoia and chronic boredom, then my admittedly stretched syllogism might suggest that *sometimes* up to one in four people will suffer from chronic boredom. If that's the case then boredom is experienced much more frequently than people are willing to allow.

* * *

Boredom and the rather awful company that it keeps seem to be far more widespread than might have been imagined. No small wonder, then, that people have persistently tried to escape chronic boredom and its malign associates.

In the late 1930s the psychologist Joseph Ephraim Barmack, then a professor at the City College of New York, was amongst the first psychologists to study boredom in a laboratory setting.

He believed that boredom resembled sleepiness and that escape from this sleepiness required stimulation. Barmack discovered that stimulants reduced the effects of fatigue, sleepiness, inattention and boredom during the performance of extremely repetitive tasks. If low arousal and insufficient motivation were the problem, money, Barmack found, served to mitigate those effects amongst his student volunteers. He also discovered that the worst effects of repetitive tasks could be blunted by the use of amphetamines, ephedrine and caffeine. Today these sorts of experiments would be banned by ethics committees, but in the 1930s Barmack was able to prove that drugs alleviated the most unpleasant aspects of the boredom of the assembly line.

I once knew a very talented specialist in the history of medieval hydraulics who worked in a history department in an Antipodean university. The French loved his work despite the fact that he lived in the southern hemisphere. The problem was that medieval hydraulics bored Stan to tears. Not surprisingly he was one of the very few people who knew anything about this unusual subject, and was exceptionally good at explaining it. Stan was invited to write book after book and article after article. They were even translated into French. Being a polite fellow with a taste for tenure, he kept on writing about medieval hydraulics.

I haven't seen Stan for years. Last time I did he was sweeping out of a bar and taking three tables with him. He was a terrible drunk, like many talented but chronically bored academics. Inebriation, it seems to me now, was the only way that he could escape from the tedium of his work. It's a common way to shake off chronic boredom. Barmack demonstrated this with his application of amphetamines. Chronic boredom drove Jack Torrance, among other things, to drink. But a really intriguing link between inebriation and the escape from boredom is offered by, of all things, the British Raj. The Reverend William Tennant reminisced on this topic in Edinburgh in 1803 in his *Indian Recreations*. In that interesting volume he observed of eighteenth-century life in the subcontinent that 'alcohol and narcotics provided an escape from boredom, frustration, and the trials of the climate. The same recreations had been part of Indian court life for centuries, although the women relaxing elegantly on a terrace, with a huqqa [hookah] give no hint of these excesses.'

There is a discussion of the theme by Jeffrey Auerbach in his article 'Imperial Boredom'. It's hard to tell whether we should believe the colonial administrators' protestations of boredom – they seem to be made more for form than for anything else – but Auerbach argues that life in the Raj was every bit as boring as the Reverend Tennant maintains. He quotes an amusing and (he believes) typical poem by a clerk of the India House:

> From ten to eleven, at breakfast at seven;
> From eleven to noon, to begin 'twas too soon;
> From twelve to one, asked 'What's to be done?'
> From one to two, found nothing to do;
> From two to three, began to foresee
> That from three to four would be a damned bore.

Foreign shores clearly offered little in the way of stimulation for these unfortunate Englishmen, yet travel remains one of the most popular cures for chronic boredom. Ivan Goncharov, who really is the sage on all matters relating to boredom, noticed the connection, although his immutably supine Oblomov would never rouse himself actually to go anywhere. The terminally bored eponymous hero is speaking with his friend Penkin:

> He fell silent suddenly, stood still for a moment, yawned, and slowly lay down on the couch.
> Both lapsed into silence.
> 'What do you read then?' asked Penkin.
> 'Me? Oh, books of travel mostly.'

There is a small literature on this strange topic of boredom and travel, subsumed under the odd label of dromomania. That word means something like a mania for locomotion. When Forrest took off on that long run of his, criss-crossing the US with a band of straggling devotees in the film *Forrest Gump*, he was probably suffering from dromomania. This illness is also called pathological tourism. Dromomaniacs display an uncontrollable and persistent desire to hurry off to some other distant place.

Ian Hacking wrote a wonderful but curiously neglected book on dromomania entitled *Mad Travellers*. Pathological tourism, Hacking explains, had its heyday in France between 1886 and 1909, when it became something of an epidemic. Known in psychiatric circles as fugue or dromomania during these twenty-three years, it was the subject of many medical disquisitions in France, Italy, then finally in Germany. Interest seems to have petered out, however, by the time 'alienists and the neurologists met [for a congress] in Nantes, 2–8 August 1909'. Professor Hacking believes that short-lived psychic epidemics like dromomania are reserved for what he calls 'transient mental illnesses'. By that he means a mental illness that 'appears at a time, in a place, and later fades away'. It is intriguing that dromomania was most popular in what was one of the most boredom-obsessed of all eras.

The most famous dromomaniac in medical history was a French gas fitter, Jean-Albert Dadas, and he came from what Hacking sees as the homeland of pathological tourism, Bordeaux. In 1886 Dadas was admitted to the Saint-André Hospital, exhausted and bewildered, after one of his journeys. He was treated, then written up in the medical thesis (entitled *Les Aliénés Voyageurs – The Mad Travellers*) of a mature student, Philippe Tissié. (*The Mad Travellers* marked the beginning of the mania both for performing and recording dromomania.) Dadas' amnesiac travels were nothing short of astonishing. His greatest began after he deserted the French army near Mons in 1881. He headed east through Prague, Berlin (he was attacked savagely by a dog while begging in East Prussia but could remember nothing of it), Posen, then Moscow. His timing was dreadful, for the czar had just been assassinated. The nihilists were to blame, and Dadas was taken for one and jailed. Luckily for him three months later the prisoners were split into three groups. The first was to be hanged, the second to be sent to Siberia, and the third group was to be marched from Moscow into exile in Turkey. Dadas, along with his nihilists and a band of alarmingly promiscuous gypsies, was placed in the third group and marched by sword-wielding Cossack guards to the border nearest Constantinople. There the sympathetic French consul funded Dadas' repatriation, at least as far as Vienna, where he took up gas fitting again. He was still amnesiac. No wonder that romantic tales like this, popularized in Philippe Tissié's thesis, triggered an epidemic. Pathological tourism took off.

At first glance, pathological tourism doesn't seem to have much to do with boredom. But I'm not so sure. It has always seemed to me to be remarkable that dromomania took root at the very time when writing and complaining about chronic boredom were at their peak in Europe. When I run through the dates of some of this book's most prominent exemplars of chronic boredom – Böcklin's *Odysseus and Calypso* (1883), Ibsen's *Hedda Gabler* (1890), Frederic Leighton's *Solitude* (1890), Edvard Munch's *Melancholy* (1896) – it is clear that Jean-Albert Dadas was on the march at the very same time that they were swooning and writing and painting and complaining. It seems that fads like dromomania need an 'environmental niche' (Ian Hacking's phrase) if they are to take off. The second half of the nineteenth century certainly provided that niche, with its fascination with all things related to boredom.

Strangely, dromomania seems to have been restricted to Europe. It never did kick off in the United States. I don't think this was because the Americans were immune to boredom. Far from it. Perhaps the Americans were saved because the USA developed different forms of pathological tourism, which displaced Europe's mental illness with colonial racism.

Drapetomania, for example, was, according to the physician Samuel A. Cartwright, a mental illness that caused black slaves to attempt to escape captivity. He put this bizarre view in a paper delivered to the Medical Association of Louisiana and repeated it in his article 'Diseases and Peculiarities of the Negro Race' (*New Orleans Medical and Surgical Journal* [1851]: 691–715). The alarming medication for this form of pathological tourism was a good whipping. Another type of pathological tourism was termed thalassophilia, love of the sea or, as it was coined by the US eugenicist Charles B. Davenport in *Heredity in Relation to Eugenics* (1911), 'sea lust'. It's a genetic, or I should say, eugenic trait – as Davenport dolefully denied it to black people – which, according to the author, is possessed by the best naval officers. Eugenicism, of course, is a mini-step from overt racism. In this case it literally drives the best races boldly on to the sea. I suspect that the reason for this was that they were bored with their families and the tedium of shore life.

The Italian novelist Alberto Moravia picks up the theme of dromomania in his novel *Boredom* (1960). The narrator, Dino, offers a very interesting and funny essay on boredom near the beginning of the book. Dino claims that he suffers what this book has termed existential boredom. But his feckless father was the victim, in Dino's eyes, of what I've been calling chronic boredom. Dino's father was bored with his wife and with family life. They were like a cage for him, and caused him to develop something resembling cabin fever. Forthwith he would borrow money from his wife and set off on his travels time after time. He perished eventually in the Sea of Japan when his ferryboat was overturned by a violent gust of wind.

Dino's mother thought that her husband suffered from more than chronic boredom: she diagnosed dromomania. This was evident not just in his ceaseless travels, but also in his enthusiasm for stamp collecting and for geography, with all their associations with foreign lands. I wonder if Dino's mother was correct; Dino believed that his father's boredom was 'the ordinary kind of boredom . . . that asks no more than to be relieved by new and unusual sensations'.

Travel is one way to escape boredom. Trying anything new will usually suffice. For sufferers of chronic boredom, more often than not that will entail some form or another of breaking the rules. Rules represent the old and the stale and the boring – sameness, predictability, confinement and middle-class life. Often this rule breaking deliberately aims to shock.

Popular culture is littered with examples of this process of rule breaking as a way to escape the chronic boredom of modern life. The problem with this rule breaking is that it so quickly becomes predictable, prosaic and boring. Avant-garde art and rock'n'roll, to take two examples, both staged revolts against the status quo precisely by way of dazzling, intense novelty, but both quickly became as predictable as corn niblets. Blue jeans, once an icon of rumbustious working-class individualism, are now worn in order for their wearer to fit into the crowd. Blue-jeaned, leather-jacketed, middle-aged, conservative white men in basements world wide form guitar bands whose monikers are derived from the First Nations or biker groups, and, in between arthritic riffs, light beer and sessions on Facebook, talk dirty. They're breaking out. And they're about as surprising as the Rolling Stones or those thousands of IKEA prints of abstract expressionist art sold the world over. The American artist Duane Hanson claimed that boredom and the banal were features of modern life. They are certainly intimately linked.

Breaking the rules and wanting to shock are often designed to assert individualism, but, as Lars Svendsen observes in his *A Philosophy of Boredom*, 'when individualism is conformist, conformism also becomes individualist'. Tattoos, outside of prison or the armed forces, were once a clear symbol of a nonconformist attitude, but everyone seems to have one now. I've seen one tattoo of the words 'Libertee' etched on a woman's bosom. The proclamation is profoundly individualist and, given its position, implies sexual rule breaking. But the medium and the sentiment have become tedious. What the rule breaking is trying to do is to reintroduce contours into the predictable and boring plateaus of middle-class modern life. In my opinion, it would be more transgressive, less predictable and far less boring to have a tattoo above the left pectoral asserting 'I Love My Mum'. Or better, your first name tattooed on your forehead. That would not be boring at all and it would be terribly useful at social gatherings.

Rule breaking, if it's done regularly, quickly becomes just another element in the edifice of the middle-class boredom that it was designed to replace. Worse still, rule breaking becomes confused with fashion and being modern and that quickly becomes old-fashioned too. Remember what Oscar Wilde had to say? 'Nothing is so dangerous as being too modern; one is apt to grow old-fashioned quite suddenly.'

Emma Bovary has a lot to answer for. Flaubert's novel, *Madame Bovary* (1857; published two years before Goncharov's *Oblomov*) paints an Emma in instinctive revolt against the chronic boredom of the conformist and rule-ridden lower-level bourgeois life of the nineteenth-century northern French provinces. The novel provides an early model for the type of individualist enthusiasm for rule breaking that I've been discussing. For Emma, rule breaking is aimed at escape and the rules she broke were sexual.

Emma marries Charles Bovary, a doctor who practises in a rural village, Tostes. She is his second wife. The romantic Emma is quickly and chronically bored by her new conformist life and by the dull Charles. The birth of her daughter, Berthe, and moving to Yonville near Rouen, do nothing to relieve her boredom. So she begins a relationship with a young law clerk, Léon, who also finds Yonville-l'Abbaye a 'very dull place'. He soon leaves to complete his law studies in Paris, and Emma's boredom becomes acute. She begins a new affair with Rodolphe, a local landowner, who is quickly 'disgusted and bored' with the relationship. Léon reappears in Rouen, but even in this revived relationship boredom intervenes. Reflecting on her liaison with Léon, Emma wonders why 'each smile hid a yawn of weariness' and why 'there was no pleasure without subsequent disgust'. By this point she has borrowed too much money for the pursuit of her romance. Rodolphe and Léon will not help. Emma resorts successfully to poison. Charles, bereft, widowed and broke, soon perishes and their daughter is left to a vile life of penury. That's the price of chronic boredom. Charles and Emma Bovary should both have taken the Boredom Proneness Scale test before they attempted to cohabit.

A small part of what Flaubert seems to be saying in his enthralling novel is that rule breaking doesn't really work. Chronic boredom bodes no good. Sex offers no decent escape. Furthermore, like Jack Torrance, Emma Bovary was underemployed. Not even her own daughter filled her time, for she was put out to a wet-nurse, the carpenter's wife Madame Rollet, soon after birth. Now I don't think that Flaubert was for one minute concerned with unemployment or even with wet-nursing. But he does make clear that Emma's mother-in-law blames her troubles in Yonville on 'a thoroughly idle life' and suggests manual work as a cure for her malaise. Emma illustrates just what can happen to a person with too little to do in their life.

Sex, to put it crassly, was Emma Bovary's escape route from boredom. And sex remains the most popular way to break the rules, to shock, and to banish boredom. It allows us 'libertee'. But the problem with sex as an escape from boredom is that it gets boring too. Perhaps it didn't for Emma Bovary, though she does begin to complain about her couplings with Léon. She perished too soon. Sexual rule breaking is directed against the boring conformity – in the eyes of the rule breaker – of modern society. If boredom flattens the contours of life, dramatic and shocking activity – usually of a sexual nature – can restore some of its highs and lows. It can get the dopamine flowing. But the desire for shocking and transgressive experience is nowadays viewed as so normal that it is hard to see it as an alternative to anything. Sex has pervaded our whole society.

It has become about as shocking as a coffee on Sundays in Starbucks. As the late Australian psychologist and social commentator, Ronald Conway, once observed: 'ours could be the first century in history to turn media-heated sexuality into a universal bore'.

Boredom – which according to the management specialist Cynthia Fisher means 'a pervasive lack of interest in and difficulty [with] concentrating on the current activity' – got the better of Goncharov's beguiling behemoth of boredom, Oblomov, and his sex drive:

> Still he never surrendered entirely to a pretty woman and never became her slave or even a faithful admirer, if only because intimacy with a woman involves a great deal of trouble. Oblomov confined himself mostly to expressing his admiration from afar, from a respectable distance.

Oblomov's solution, a surrender to uninterest, may seem preferable to tiring and trying transgression.

Of course not everyone wants to escape from chronic boredom and its often unpleasant companions. Boredom can become for some people a chosen way of life. I once had a very brilliant friend, Kevin, who, despite his brains, was also quite attractive to both sexes. For reasons that I have never understood, he consistently complained that he wished to escape from the prying eyes of the world – sexually, intellectually, socially, and even physically. The whole works. He told me once that he was planning to maim himself by dropping a large rock on his slender right shin, and that he hoped the whole right leg might be chopped off as a result. Maiming, he thought, would render him invisible and would thus enable him to live the dreary, private, safe and utterly boring life he craved. I thought this was utterly preposterous. I told him that the legless usually drew a lot of attention to themselves. But he would have none of this. Boredom, he insisted, is good.

Kevin wasn't the first person ever to have felt this. There is a medical condition that is called apotemnophilia: the burning desire to have a limb removed. Unsurprisingly, it's relatively rare. Goodness knows what drove Kevin, or any of the other apotemnophiliacs like him, to think in this way. But a variety of theories for apotemnophilia have been adduced. Sometimes it is termed a paraphilia, or sexual fetish. This seems to be the view of John Money, the Johns Hopkins University psychology professor who discovered the illness. Others argue that its attraction is linked to self-identity: the sufferer had always envisaged himself as limbless. It's certainly the case that some apotemnophiliacs have psychiatric problems. Still others view it as a transient mental illness, not unlike the dromomania from which Jean-Albert Dadas suffered. The strangest explanation comes from a 2009 study by Paul McGeoch and his colleagues: 'apotemnophilia is a neurological disorder that arises from a dysfunction of the right parietal [brain] lobe'. To believe that, I suspect, is to believe anything. But I wonder if the simplest reason for an enthusiasm for apotemnophilia might be Kevin's explanation: a desire to escape from normal life and from the need for achievement and success. To embrace the boring life, that's to say, is to don the cloak of invisibility.

I am glad to say that Kevin never did maim himself. Instead he became a very successful court lawyer and one with an admirably strong social conscience. But he never lost his desire for boring anonymity either. Like Hydraulics Stan he ended up drinking a lot, and finding his anonymity and escape that way – legless, but in a much more traditional and acceptable manner than by apotemnophilia.

But not all boredom is of this dopamine-driven, chronic variety. Much of the time simple boredom comes and it goes. And much of the time *choice* enables us to expunge the emotion. But sometimes choice is not an option. What happens, then, when boredom becomes prolonged and unavoidable?

3

Humans, animals and incarceration

Work is not a problem. I work in a school.

I teach children.

I teach them:

1 Routine

2 When to keep their mouths shut

3 How to put up with boredom . . .

JOY STONE, A lonely 27-year-old drama teacher who lives near Glasgow, makes this desolate list in Janice Galloway's 1989 novel on depression, *The Trick is to Keep Breathing*. Anorexic and clinically depressed, to survive her illness Joy has to learn to deal with the simplest and most inevitable things in life. Boredom is one of them. Children too need to hone their skills while still young. They need to be taught how to cope with an emotion that they'll surely encounter many times during their lives. Being able to put up with boredom is part of their process of learning how to fit in, Joy Stone seems to be saying.

Very small children can be bored despite their not being able to name the emotion from which they are suffering. Boredom is clearly not the sole prerogative of articulate and self-reflective adults. So, when the psychiatrist Erich Fromm asserts in *The Sane Society* (1955) that 'man is the only animal that can be bored', it's hard not to be sceptical. Boredom does not need to be understood as one of the defining characteristics of what it is to be human. If small or large inarticulate humans can experience boredom, along with a whole host of other social emotions, how then can we deny them to other animals? This does sound like a bizarre supposition, I'll admit. But animal behaviour researchers such as Frans de Waal, Françoise Wemelsfelder and Marc Bekoff treat it very seriously. They have no doubts that animals can experience emotions such as boredom. Wemelsfelder and Bekoff suggest that they can get bored for the very same reasons that you do: too much of the same thing and too little stimulation.

The sort of boredom that an animal feels is, naturally, the simple sort rather than the existential malaise. Most people who have kept animals have often witnessed them being bored. They sleep more and when they are awake they harass you for games or walks. And when you don't take them for walks or to play games they begin to slope about the house or the yard in a disconsolate fashion. They mope and they droop and they are listless. Why, then, is it so easy to raise the hackles of scientists and of psychologists and of philologists, if you make the claim that animals experience boredom? What's behind the vehemence of their denial? Are animal owners so completely mistaken? Can't they recognize the same symptoms in animals as they do in young children, or in themselves?

Animals don't talk. That's the problem. This gives the sceptics – those who deny such emotions to animals – a real advantage in a debate like this. An older child can say they are bored, despite the fact that they may be wrong: the German psychiatrist Otto Fenichel maintained that children often label excitement as boredom. This is because they confuse boredom with restlessness and jitteriness. But a *very* small child or an animal can't speak at all. Lurking behind their unfortunate aphasia, furthermore, is an old furphy: that an emotion which cannot be enunciated or named cannot be felt. It makes denying boredom to animals even more convincing.

It was the ancient Greek philosopher Aristotle, I believe, who first made this link between feeling and saying. The argument is often taken one step further: from speech to self-consciousness. Aristotle rejected the possibility that animals and small children could experience the emotion of happiness. They are not capable of performing the activities (which he terms 'noble acts') that he believes endow humans with happiness. To perform these activities a person needs to be quite conscious of what they're doing and to be able to enunciate it, which animals and the very young cannot. This is what Aristotle says in his *Nichomachean Ethics*:

We have good reasons therefore for not speaking of an ox or horse or any other animal as being happy, because none of these is able to participate in noble activities. For this cause also children cannot be happy, for they are not old enough to be capable of noble acts; when children are spoken of as happy, it is a compliment for their promise to the future. (1099b30)

This viewpoint was taken over by the Stoics, to a degree, and has passed down circuitously into the drearily optimistic culture of the Protestant Enlightenment. But it makes little sense, for if children can't be happy, then they can't experience any other primary emotion, such as sadness, fear, anger, surprise or disgust. That's unless happiness is a special emotion that is superior to the others I have just mentioned – but of course it is not. Primary emotions have their adaptive and Darwinian role in that they help creatures to survive and to flourish; without them, they would not. Neither age, maturity nor self-consciousness has anything to do with the ability to experience the primary emotions.

According to most research into early childhood children begin to feel the more complex social emotions – such as sympathy, embarrassment, shame, guilt, pride, jealousy, envy, gratitude, admiration, indignation or contempt – from a very early age. Unlike the primary emotions, these social emotions probably do take some of their impetus from self-consciousness. Jerome Kagan and Antonio Damasio point out that children seem to have a sense of self – self-consciousness, if you like – by about eighteen months. That's well before they develop the capacity for language. It's likely, therefore, that small children have the ability to experience the social emotions well before they can utter the first person pronoun, which used to be taken as the marker of self-consciousness. The emotion of boredom, the first cousin of disgust, must enter the child's mindscape early too.

And perhaps animals' mindscapes as well. The 30-year-old chimp, Santino, from the Furuvik Zoo in Sweden collects rocks in his enclosure before the zoo opens and places them on the visitor-facing side of his island. From his carefully planned cache he hurls his missiles at the visitors. Animals are not supposed to be able to plan consciously for the future. Santino's actions, according to Mathias Osvath of the University of Lund, suggest an unexpected level of self-consciousness: 'It implies they [the chimps] have a highly developed consciousness, including life-like mental simulations of days to come. I would guess that they plan much of their everyday behaviour.'

Santino's rock throwing could imply some of the social emotions. It's not hard to see how a sense of wounded pride, indignation and envy of these hairless chimps roaming free might have made him so irritable. Could boredom be added to the list? I'd really like to think that Santino becomes so fed up with being gawped at by three hundred visitors per day that he's taken to seeking relief by throwing rocks at them.

Self-consciousness and the capacity to experience the social emotions must differ from whales to dolphins to crayfish. Although not all animals can possess the same capacity to experience emotion and self-consciousness, some animals, like Santino, may have an unexpectedly high level of self-consciousness and, related to this, an unexpectedly high capacity to experience social emotions such as boredom. There's nothing magical or elitist about such social emotions.

Frans de Waal, in his famous *Chimpanzee Politics* lists, amongst other beneficial emotions, the following as having been experienced by his band of primates: sympathy, reciprocity, jealousy and friendship, along with such emotional registers as self-awareness and triadic awareness. The biological function of all of these emotions, as neurologists like Damasio insist, is to protect life. They fend off dangers and they can facilitate social relations in such a way as to assist in both the flourishing and the protection of organisms.

And finally something that was touched on in the first chapter and which relates to the cognitive understanding of emotion: the cognitivists, such as David Konstan, believe that human emotion, because it involves both a reactive and an evaluative element, cannot be shared by animals. Cats and dogs lack the evaluative capacity possessed by human beings. I'd make two points here. First, the status of the evaluative capacity of many animals is not clear at all. If, as Mathias Osvath claims, Santino has a high level of consciousness, then perhaps he does possess this evaluative capacity. Which other animals could possess this capacity – gorillas, wolves, dolphins, whales? And what of small children? When does their evaluative capacity kick in? At eighteen months, at four years of age, at seven? It's not certain. The second point relates to how this evaluative capacity operates. Presumably it must begin at the very same instant as the reactive response. Or does this learned element of emotion begin a few seconds later than the reactive element? (You experience disgust at the mouldy tofu, then a few seconds later you throw up your arms or furrow your brow.) If there is a cognitive lag, then, is the real emotion the reactive or the evaluative element? I would suspect it is the former, the one that humans and animals can share.

When the experience of boredom is denied in animals it is probably because, quite reasonably, it seems preposterous that an orang-utan should feel the same emotions as, for example, Robert Burton, the learned seventeenth-century author of *The Anatomy of Melancholy* (1621), one of the greatest of English books on chronic depression and existential boredom. But I wonder if this does not point to another problem as well: the confusion between simple boredom and existential boredom. To suggest that animals suffer existential boredom is of course a little extreme. But maybe the confusion of the two forms of boredom really does colour the argument. Animals aren't 'allowed' boredom because of its purportedly cerebral nature. Existential boredom, for so many thinkers, has come to be seen as one of the costs, or even the badges, of modernity or civilization, both conditions to which non-human animals do not have access. Animals can neither talk nor write of boredom. Could it be that the ability to enunciate existential boredom is part of the prerequisite for feeling it? Simple boredom, on the other hand, *can* be felt without the ability to name it. Just because a gibbon cannot tell us that she is bored does not provide any support for the argument that she is never bored. It simply means, as I have said, that she can't talk English or French. *C'est tout.*

Boredom is a condition of the socialized and, for much of the time, of the well fed. There are of course exceptions – Andy Warhol was very skinny and he claimed that he was very bored indeed. But it is probably different for animals. The better fed they are, I suspect, the more liable they are to boredom. And it is no doubt true that dogs living with humans get more bored than dogs that live in the wild, perhaps because pet dogs don't need to spend so long foraging for food. They have more opportunity for boredom; more leisure, that is to say. It looks a little as if humans cause domesticated animals to feel boredom simply because they like them so much. It is also possible that lonely animals in captivity have a higher expectation of stimulation and if this is not addressed they become prone to boredom.

More substantial conclusions concerning the nature of boredom in animals have been reached by the animal psychologists Françoise Wemelsfelder and Marc Bekoff. Just as in humans, it's the product of predictability and confinement. In most animal cases the confinement is literal: in a cage or on a chain. Wemelsfelder likes to describe boredom as the experience of 'impaired voluntary attention'. She believes that, in situations of confinement (such as prisons, hospital wards, 'or even schools'), voluntary attention, the opportunity that is for voluntary interaction with one's surroundings, is impeded. Boredom follows. Wemelsfelder believes that the reaction in confined animals is comparable to that in confined humans. Sustained confinement produces in animals, initially, a real and observable sense of boredom. This is followed by frustration, agitation, anger, violence and, eventually, depression. The confined animal moves from boredom to a manic response (being agitated and angry) to a depressive one. The process, Wemelsfelder believes, matches the reactions of humans. It provides a systematic way to think about boredom for both animals and humans. Boredom does not *cause* angry or even manic behaviour, nor depression; instead it is one link in the chain of an affective process that can begin with prolonged confinement, solitude and sensory deprivation. Boredom, as I argued in the last chapter, keeps company with these emotional states. It is not causative of them. It can represent the first element of a process which may include, sequentially, anger and depression.

Dr Wemelsfelder draws on the justly famous paper, 'The Psychology of Boredom' by Otto Fenichel. Its Freudian elements do not interest Wemelsfelder; what does is Fenichel's distinction between normal boredom and pathological boredom, the latter understood more precisely by Wemelsfelder as anger and depression. She suggests that unrelieved boredom may readily shift into these more damaging states. The process is illustrated in some detail in a variety of her articles.

A lonely, locked-up animal will at first sink into a state of simple boredom. If captivity is prolonged, that quickly mutates into what Otto Fenichel identified as the pathological phase of the emotion. The animal behaves in a very strange manner. A dog raised in isolation until the age of 16 to 32 weeks, for example, whirls, paces, and can exhibit bizarre postures. Stereotypic behaviour like this is the first reaction to a too predictable environment. Wemelsfelder observes that 'as animals stay longer in their cages . . . they may lick, suck, or chew the bars of their cages or start pecking, sucking, or chewing their cage mates' bodies . . . [they may pluck] fur or feather or . . . [chew] their own limbs, genitals, tail; they may also eat their own excrement or regurgitate and reingest previous meals'. Angry and manic behaviour soon seems to set in, which can lead to the animal turning in on itself like this poor bored, self-immolating cockatoo. This is 'displacement preening', a type of redirected behaviour that results from the boredom brought on by excessive confinement and solitude. These birds should never be in cages.

In such a situation, Wemelsfelder reveals, an animal can react by performing 'self-mutilation or it can become passive, sometimes maintaining motionlessness, so called "drowsy" postures for a long time'. Tethered sows and fattening pigs spend long periods, up to six hours, of motionless 'sitting', often

16 Self-immolating cockatoo

with their head hanging down, or pressed against stall divisions. The restless behaviour seems to subside and, as Wemelsfelder states, 'eventually, chronically bored animals may give up looking for things to do; they may stop resisting monotony, give in to lethargy, and become helpless and depressed'.

But most of the studies on the effects of incarceration on animals fail to mention boredom: they go straight from the clinking shut of the cage to the animals' fear, agitation and depression. I suppose they ignore the inevitable initial boredom felt by animals because it seems too trivial to emphasize, or because it appears to be just a transitory and inconsequential phase leading to behaviour that is more worthy of study. But, as Wemelsfelder stresses, boredom is in and of itself a significant stage in many animals' appalling experience of incarceration.

Stuart Grassian, in a pair of papers, summarized research findings on the effects of isolation and confinement on animals, including aggressive behaviour in mice, cognitive impairment and symptoms in adult rhesus monkeys, and isolation-produced fear in dogs. More recent research has found that bad incarceration of primates is linked to a permanent alteration in the way that their brains work. Brains, as Norman Doidge explains in *The Brain that Changes Itself*, are very plastic organs: they can be remapped. Incarceration therefore is not just bad luck for the monkeys, but also for the research. It's poor science to use deformed research subjects, quite aside from any consideration of the ethical implications of treating another creature in this fashion.

Stuart Grassian's much-read papers on the effects of solitary confinement on Massachusetts prisoners traced a direct connection between an emotional state shared by humans and animals – boredom – and mental illness. Boredom, to follow Françoise Wemelsfelder, seems to be an early warning signal of more deleterious conditions that are liable to follow. These, as Grassian also makes clear, can entail anger or mania or depression. It's as if boredom sits at the still point between the bipolar extremes.

J.M. Barbalet, in an interesting sociological study entitled 'Boredom and Social Meaning', maintained that 'depression is . . . inwardly directed to the self, boredom more typically outwardly directed to activity, engagements, environment'. Surprisingly, this apparently unlikely connection is played out far away from the laboratory, in Jane Austen's *Emma* (1816). Although the word 'boredom' is not used in the novel ('ennui' is, however) more than one critic has suggested that it's boredom that drives Emma's restless matchmaking.

Life for 21-year-old Emma is very boring. With her mother dead, her sister married and her close friend Miss Taylor just wed, all she has for company is her genial, but selfish and hypochondriac father. Early in the novel, Austen speaks of 'many a long October and November evening [that] must be struggled through' for Emma and her father. The well nourished pair, incarcerated in their predictable, lonely and narrow routines, are waiting for Christmas and for the arrival of Emma's sister and her children and, with them, a temporary reprieve from their tedious life. Their estate, Hartfield, the wealthiest in the district, is a large-scale and pampered version of a cockatoo's cage.

An inveterate self-coddler, everything is 'inwardly directed to the self' with Mr Woodhouse. No surprise, then, if Barbalet had diagnosed him with depression. The emulous Mrs Elton hits on this too when she suggests to Emma that Bath 'is so cheerful a place, that it could not fail of being of use to Mr Woodhouse's spirits, which, I understand are sometimes much depressed'. Perhaps Mr Woodhouse represents an image of what could become of Emma if she does not find a remedy for the boredom of the secluded life that they share. No wonder that for relief Emma turns 'outside', as Barbalet would say, to matchmaking. It represents for her a kind of a psychological dromomania. Mr Woodhouse and his daughter illustrate very plainly the instability of boredom, and how it may slide over into depression if simple boredom persists and finds no remedy.

The Woodhouses' confinement may have been more psychological than strictly physical, but what of those unfortunates who are actually incarcerated? It's not only scientists' rhesus monkeys who are kept behind bars. Stuart Grassian's powerful arguments on the nature of solitary confinement make a consideration of the role of boredom in prisons inevitable. Some sense of the experience of incarceration can be drawn from the autobiographical writing of the popular novelist and one-time politician, Jeffrey Archer, who described his stint in prison in a best-selling trilogy, *Belmarsh: Hell* (2002), *Wayland: Purgatory* (2003), and *Heaven: A Prison Diary* (2004).

The experience of prison must have been especially difficult for a man like Jeffrey Archer. He'd achieved prominence and wealth as a successful writer and politician during the years of Margaret Thatcher's government. He became Deputy

Chairman of the Conservative Party in 1984 and a life peer in 1991. Archer came to grief, and to prison, when he perjured himself over an alleged assignation with the prostitute Monica Coghlan. He went to prison in 2001 and was released 725 days later on Monday 21 July 2003. It was a spectacular, deeply embarrassing, and very public fall.

'Prison is a grim contrast with the luxurious life he forfeited when he was convicted of perjury last year,' wrote Jeevan Vasagar and Michael White in the *Guardian* eleven days before Archer's release, quoting the peer's own descriptions of life inside:

'At noon, I'm let out of the cell to join the queue for lunch. One look at what is on offer and I can't face it – overcooked meat, heaven knows from which animal, mushy peas swimming in water and potatoes that Oliver Twist would have rejected.' Lord Archer discovers that life inside offers less glittering attractions than shepherd's pie and Krug; prisoners hold ant races to relieve the boredom, with the losing ants ending up 'in tomorrow's soup'.

Some of Archer's fellow inmates would have been in and out of prison more times than the peer had popped a bottle of Krug. But it seems that even they had not become accustomed to its boring rigours. Boredom bulks large in Lord Archer's prison narrative. He is open about it. He is emphatic that 'the biggest enemy I have to contend with is boredom, and it's a killer'. Of his life inside, Archer knows that 'boredom will become my greatest challenge'.

Christmas is the worst day of the year for those who are banged up, Archer says. And, 'for prisoners who do not return to work, Boxing Day is almost worse'. Weekends, for the same reason, seem particularly hard to bear; 'Weekends are deadly in a prison . . . a lot of prisoners just remain in bed'. Sleep, then, is one way to kill time. There are others. On one occasion several inmates join him to clean the prison infirmary: 'You may well ask why Carl and Jason helped me with the spring clean. Boredom. The spring clean killed a morning for all of us.' Lord Archer is especially horrified at the scale of drug taking in prisons, although at times he comes close to seeing it as just another of the solutions for the never-ending boredom.

What does Archer do to kill time? 'I'm lucky,' he tells us, 'because I have my writing to occupy me.' And write he certainly does. During his 725 days of incarceration he wrote, amongst other things, the three volumes of prison diaries, one novel, one book of short stories and one screenplay. But it's still not enough. He confesses that, despite his writing, 'many aspects of prison life are unbearable: boredom, confinement, missing family and friends', and he refers to life in the Hollesley Bay prison, his final place of incarceration, as 'those lifeless hours'. If Lord Archer had had fewer internal resources he might well have ended up like one of Françoise Wemelsfelder's lonely caged animals and become subject to acute depression. That he did not may have been the result of his writing.

The German architect Albert Speer had a fall as spectacular as that of Jeffrey Archer. But Speer's was vastly more protracted and I dare say more deserved. Before his prison term, Speer seems to have had the most boredom-free of lives. He had acted as Hitler's chief architect before he became, for a portion of the Second World War, a successful Minister of Armaments and War Production for the Third Reich. After the defeat of Germany Speer was tried at Nuremberg. He was sentenced to twenty years in prison for assisting the Nazi regime, for war crimes and for crimes against humanity. Speer and six other fellow Nazi officials were incarcerated on 18 July 1947 in Spandau Prison in what was to become West Berlin. In the early years of his sentence Albert Speer was kept in solitary confinement for all but half an hour a day. He was not permitted to address either the guards or the other prisoners. This savage regime was eventually relaxed, at least by all of the guards except for the Russian contingent. But Speer's isolation, over the course of his sentence, became all the more severe: he was viewed by the six other fellow Nazi detainees as an outcast because he had publicly apologized and accepted responsibility for his crimes as an agent of the Third Reich.

Speer composed a best-selling prison diary – published in English as *Spandau: The Secret Diaries* (1976) – based on the letters to his children that had been smuggled out of Spandau. The same emphasis on the awfulness of boredom in prison can be found in Speer's diary as in that of Jeffrey Archer. In a famous passage Speer notes: '*September 11, 1949* Another six weeks have passed. One month after another. Somewhere I have read that boredom is the torment of hell that Dante forgot.' That boredom was part of the intended punishment is clear from the imposition of the strictest form of solitary confinement. Like Archer, Speer states again and again that he wrote to combat the boredom of his incarceration. Speer seems to have slipped into a depressed state of mind while in prison although the diaries may have saved him from the worst effects. But his diaries did nothing to curb some exceptionally bizarre behaviour.

Albert Speer reports that one remedy for boredom was a make-believe dromomania, a remarkable version of the same strange sickness that plagued Albert Dadas in the previous chapter. Speer of course couldn't travel anywhere, but he did adapt his daily exercise in the prison yard to fit the model of pathological tourism. By carefully measuring the path round the yard he determined to walk the distance from Berlin to Heidelberg. 'This project,' he writes, 'is a training of the will, a battle against endless boredom.' The idea expanded to extravagant proportions: an imaginary journey all around the world, achieved of course within the limited space of the prison yard. Stickler for detail that he was, Speer planned his journey from guidebooks, maps and encyclopaedias, and calculated every yard travelled. The journey began in Germany, swung south through Asia and upwards into Siberia whence he entered North America via the Bering Strait. This epic voyage ended just south of Guadalajara in Mexico. But even this 'senseless hike' could not cure Speer's boredom. On 3 December 1963 he recorded: 'The monotony of my days can scarcely be conveyed in those notes. The forever unchanging sameness of more than six thousand days cannot be recorded.'

Another Albert – Albert Camus – also wrote of the placatory effects of imaginary dromomania in his bewildering novel *The Outsider* (1942). Its protagonist, Meursault, is an alienated and, to my reading, feeble-minded character, who has been locked up for committing a murder on a North African beach. Awaiting execution he describes his life in solitary and tries to convince us that he's not bored:

> The main problem, once again, was killing time. I ended up not being bored at all . . . [I'd started] thinking about my room and, in my imagination, I'd set off from one corner and walk around making a mental note of everything I saw on the way. At first it didn't take very long. But every time I did it, it took a bit longer. Because I'd remember every piece of furniture . . . every object and, on every object, every detail, every mark, crack or chip, and then even the colour or the grain of the wood . . . I realized that a man who'd only lived for a day could easily live for a hundred years in prison. He'd have enough memories not to get bored.

But Meursault is not really convincing, and his imaginary dromomania takes him no further than the walls of his own cell.

Albert Speer often describes his Spandau prison cell. It wouldn't have been much larger than that shown below. It's easy to speculate on the effect that an enclosure like this would have. In his paper on the effects of solitary confinement on prisoners in a Massachusetts maximum security prison, Stuart Grassian wrote that 'incarceration in solitary caused either severe exacerbation or recurrence of pre-existing [mental] illness, or the appearance of an acute mental illness in individuals who had previously been free of any such illness'. Grassian is speaking of a form of incarceration even more severe than

17 Cell in the prison in Warren, Maine, 2002

that suffered by Speer, although the difference is presumably only one of degree. Speer had his ailments, however. On 20 February 1950 he complained that his heart was taking leaps – 'they are extrasystoles which, as a medical paper reports, can be attributed to the monotony of modern life and isolation within mass society' – and he clearly believed that boredom was to blame. But it's some testament to the strength of his internal resources (I say nothing of his politics) that, through a combination of clandestine writing, reading, dromomania and even gardening, he managed to emerge from his 'solitary' confinement and incarceration intact.

There is nothing new in the claim that boredom is a deliberate part of penal punishment. But it is a startling way of putting an emotion, so often decried as trivial and childish, to the service of a social utility, a utility that benefits no one, neither the prisoner nor the community at large. Prison life shows the danger of enforced chronic boredom. If the boredom is not remedied it will drive a person to anger and to violence, to dangerous diversions such as narcotics, and to the depression that has been the subject of this chapter. This shows what an unfortunately practical role boredom can play in modern society. Making a cockatoo out of a crook is neither a good nor a profitable thing.

The isolation and confinement of prison breeds loneliness. Jeffrey Archer claimed that one of the worst aspects of prison was 'missing family and friends'. Loneliness seems inextricably linked to boredom and to the depression which seems to flow from it. Maybe I can start to illustrate part of this connection with a brief personal anecdote. Some years ago, when a little boy named John was visiting, he announced that he was lonely. I was thunderstruck. What had happened to the poor little thing? And what should be done to solve his existential problem? Get him a cat, find him some little friends, take him to the mall? The mall seemed best. Looking for a bit of time to get ready for what I envisioned as a mission of avuncular mercy, I got out his Dinky cars and urged him to amuse himself with the toys in the interim.

When I returned, I found John absorbed in his game. He was lining his cars up in columns across the carpet just like Danny in *The Shining*. He barely noticed me. I asked him if he'd like to go out now. He looked up at me and shook his head. 'No, I'm not bored any more. I want to stay at home with my cars.' And so we did. I had been quite wrong to fear that he was troubled by a deep psychological malaise, a severe case of loneliness. The little boy was simply bored.

It's very easy to confuse boredom with loneliness. Both involve a lack of external stimuli: in the case of loneliness what's lacking is the company of people or of a specific person. This type of loneliness is situational, in much the same way as boredom could be said to be situational. The Australian anthropologist Yasmine Musharbash illustrates this neatly. She has heard the Warlpiri Aboriginal people from the Yuendumu settlement use 'boring' in the same sense as 'lonely'. She illustrates: 'At Yuendumu, if directly applied to persons, the term [boring] is always used in the active sense, so that "Millie must be boring, all alone now" meant that she must feel lonely after we had left her to travel to another settlement.' There is a considerable literature exploring the link between loneliness and boredom. Not surprisingly, this frequently takes as its focus the elderly who are resident in nursing homes.

That boredom, loneliness and depression exist in close conjunction – or even in close confusion, as we'll see – can perhaps be seen most readily in visual art. *Solitude* (1890) by the Victorian artist Lord Frederic Leighton might make this clear. The posture of this young woman recalls the description of 'poor Maria' by Laurence Sterne, 'sitting under a poplar . . . with her elbow in her lap, and her head leaning on one side within her hand – a small brook ran at the foot of the tree'.

18 Frederic Leighton, *Solitude, c.* 1890

Maria's problem was that she had been jilted by her lover, and Leighton's maid too is of the age when this malady can strike. But her posture – the right hand supporting the drooping head and her elbow bent – is typical also of boredom. Leighton's title allows for both interpretations. Is the young woman in *Solitude* bored? Why not? At her age she should have better things do than sitting and staring into a pond.

Loneliness need not just be situational, as it appears to be in Leighton's painting. It can also be experienced less specifically as a sense of loss and as a result it displays a strong connection with depression. The US writer William Deresiewicz suggests in his essay 'The End of Solitude' that loneliness is not the absence of company, but grief over its absence. It's a very telling way to think about the emotion. In his popular book, *The Age of Empathy: Nature's Lessons for a Kinder Society*, the Dutch primatologist Frans de Waal suggests that 'our bodies and our minds are made for social life, and we become hopelessly depressed in its absence. This is why next to death, solitary confinement is our worst punishment.'

De Waal provides some stark examples of the 'absence of company' to which Deresiewicz alludes. 'Bonding,' he states, 'is so good for us that the most reliable way to extend one's life expectancy is to marry and stay married. The flip side is the risk [of mortality] we run after losing a partner.' De Waal illustrates his point with the example of elephants which 'are known to return to the remains of dead companions to solemnly stand over their sun-bleached bones. They may take an hour to gently turn the bones over and over, smelling them. Sometimes they carry off bones, but other elephants have been seen returning to the "grave" site.'

One of the most compelling examinations of the link between boredom, solitude and depression is provided by Alberto Moravia. Marcello Clerici, the protagonist in Moravia's powerful wartime novel *The Conformist* (1951), is overcome by guilt because he had, he believed, shot and killed a seedy ex-priest called Lino. That man had attempted to rape Marcello as a 13-year-old. Marcello's guilt, as a child, was especially severe. He had been trying to cajole a firearm from Lino to impress his classmates, and felt complicit in his own near-rape. Marcello, once grown up, tried to assuage his guilt by living a life of dreary conformity, 'order, composure, normality' – or, in other words, a wilfully boring existence. He hankered to experience 'a sort of grey, benumbed normality', and bragged that he lived a life that is like 'a million others'. Yet Marcello's life is not normal. He is racked with loneliness, and completely removed from his fellows, even his wife and child. In the finale, Marcello breaks clear of his web of loneliness, solitude and willed boredom, but this leads to his and his family's death.

When boredom is induced and prolonged by some form or another of external trauma (such as being shut up in a cage, or denied human stimulus, or being driven by guilt to deliberately exclude oneself from the world in the case of Marcello Clerici) there follows either an angry and self-destructive reaction, or depression. It is almost as if boredom represents a compromise between these other two dangerous emotional states – a transitional point through which the sufferer travels towards the other extreme.

And perhaps this compromise state is a healthy one. Perhaps boredom acts as an early warning system designed to protect against situations which may be dangerous for psychological well-being, situations which might encourage agitation and anger and depression. Perhaps boredom increases during a repetitive and predictable experience or in situations of entrapment that it would be in our best interests to escape. Spend too long in a very boring situation, that is to say, and the feeling of irritability and restlessness inherent in the emotion may escalate and leave a person prey to the depredations of extreme agitation and anger, or depression. Surprisingly, boredom – as unpleasant as it can be – seems to be a beneficial emotion, warning us away from potentially much more damaging situations such as Marcello Clerici became incapable of avoiding.

Simple boredom plays an important role in our emotional lives. Its function as well as its biological basis have been the focus of the discussion up to this point. But what of its headier, more grown-up version, existential boredom? In one form or another it's been the subject of many books and even artworks throughout the history of literature. And that's what I'd like to look at next, the historical basis of existential boredom. What I hope to be able to show is that, unlike its simple cousin, it rests on a purely intellectual foundation.

4

The disease that wasteth at noonday

The demon of *acedia* is called the 'noonday demon'. It is the most oppressive of all demons. It attacks a hermit at about the fourth hour and besieges his soul until the eighth hour. First this demon makes the sun appear sluggish and immobile, just as if the length of the day were fifty hours. Then it causes the hermit to look continually at the windows and forces him to step out of his cell and to gaze at the sun. This is to see how far it still is from the ninth hour. And it forces him to look around, here and there, to see whether any of his brethren are near. In addition the demon makes him dislike his place, his life itself, and the work of his hands. It makes him think that he has lost the affection of his brethren and that there is no one to comfort him. If, during these days, anybody annoyed the hermit, the demon would cause this to increase his hatred. It stirs the hermit also to yearn for different places in which he can easily find what is necessary for his life and carry on a much less difficult and more profitable profession. It is not on account of the locality, the demon suggests, that one pleases God. He can be worshipped everywhere. To these thoughts the demon adds the memory of the hermit's family and of his former way of life. It highlights the paltry length of his lifetime, holding before the hermit's eyes all the hardships of his ascetic life. The demon employs all his wiles to cause the hermit to leave his cell and to flee from the racecourse of his vocation.

This passage was written by the early Christian hermit Evagrius in his *On the Eight Evil Thoughts* and it is probably the earliest detailed account of existential boredom. Acedia, the term for the monkish malaise that is described by Evagrius and many clerics to follow him, is a curious Greek word. It means something like 'indifference' or 'apathy'. In English the term has become accidie. The nickname for this strange condition, as well as for the entity that was supposed to have caused it, is the 'noonday demon' or the 'demon of noontide' or even the 'midday fiend'. That nickname comes ultimately from the ninetieth psalm (here in the beautiful Wyclif Bible version, but just slightly modernized):

His truth shall encompass thee with a shield: thou shalt not dread of the night's dread. Of an arrow flying in the day, of a goblin going in the darkness, of assailing, and a midday fiend.

But these names don't really help to show what Evagrius' monk is suffering. That's unless you really do believe that a supernatural creature, such as the noonday demon, could be responsible for what these ascetics are going through.

When Evagrius wrote his well-known description of acedia in *On the Eight Evil Thoughts*, he was a hermit himself. He was living the ascetic life in one of the scattered coenobitic communities that had sprung up in the deserts of North Africa, south of Alexandria in a region that was sometimes termed the 'Desert of Cells'. Evagrius must have seen many cases of acedia. The monk's life in these North African deserts, though full of religious edification, was monotonous, harsh and solitary. On the famous Mount Nitria, where in 383 Evagrius began his eremetic life, there were nearly 5,000 monks who, despite the heat, the dirt, the fleas, the hard beds, the bedbugs, the poisonous snakes, the lack of sleep, the shortage of decent food and the brackish water, lived and worshipped in their separate cells. The hermits shared work, meals and, on Saturdays and Sundays, worship. Apart from the work and the meals the day was silent. It's no surprise that these religious became woefully stressed and fell into dejection, restlessness, and a psychotic dislike of their grime-ridden cells and their malodorous fellow hermits. They came to experience a real disgust for their way of life. As the passage from Evagrius shows, they soon developed a lust to quit their monastic abodes altogether and to seek salvation in greener pastures. Or a demon forced them to. And they soon became very angry too.

Acedia seems to have ripped through these desert communities like a virulent disease. Little wonder that Evagrius reacts with such incomprehension and fear, desperate to understand and to apportion blame. Evagrius found his explanation in the supernatural. He saw acedia as the result of spiritual weakness on the sufferer's part. The sufferer was blameworthy, but he had also been tempted by this devil. The sufferer had not fought hard enough against the blandishments of the noonday demon. These days a psychiatrist might attribute the malaise to hysterical contagion or, in today's parlance, conversion disorder. But might it not be better understood as simple boredom?

Evagrius' reasoning appears extreme, but his intellectual world understood things far differently to ours. Evagrius had come late to this extreme and taxing way of spiritual life. As a younger man he appears to have had the least austere of experiences, for he fared well in his early years as a deacon and then as an archdeacon. He assisted Gregory of Nazienus in his combat with Arianism, which taught that Jesus Christ was not equal to God the Father, or to the Holy Spirit, but a subservient, Johnny-come-lately deity. Evagrius subsequently won a name for himself in Constantinople and, because of that renown, he understandably succumbed to the flesh: food, drink and adultery. The cure came in 383 when he entered the dusty, bug-ridden embrace of the ascetic life within the community at Nitria and then at Cellia. During these last fourteen years of his short life he composed *On the Eight Evil Thoughts*. Evagrius did not want any of his fellow monks to slip back into the fleshly pursuits that he had overcome with such difficulty.

Most people with an interest in acedia understand Evagrius' 'noonday demon' as what I have been calling existential boredom. The unhappy religious recluse described by the holy

Evagrius plays a founding role in a long tradition relating to this condition. Acedia represents what might be termed a specifically Christian existential boredom. It is the result of confronting the problem of God's plan and creation and wondering 'where do I fit into it?' The response to this query was often a sneaking suspicion that it might be 'nowhere'. And from that doleful answer follows the powerful feeling of spiritual emptiness, isolation and apathy described by Evagrius.

The tradition of acedia, with its origins in the Old Testament, runs right down through the centuries into modern secular experience. Over the centuries, the Desert Fathers' suffering in the early hours of the afternoon became the object of the attention and elaboration of monks, medical men, philosophers, and many twentieth-century novelists. Thanks to these bookish individuals acedia spread and mutated, although its biblical lineage roils constantly just beneath its contemporary literary patina.

In its modern phase, however, acedia becomes a strange conjunction of depression – or what seems to be depression – and a doubt in the goodwill of the world itself. It is said to produce a powerful and unrelieved emptiness in which the sufferer feels isolated. One experiences a loss of personal meaning. There is an absence of desire and even a difficulty in concentrating on things. These feelings, it is often said, result from the sufferer's seeing himself as an isolated individual in an essentially unsympathetic world whose customs and traditions have no relevance. As a result the sufferer feels himself to be doing meaningless work and, what is more, his life lacks meaningful leisure. The victim feels at odds with his community. It is very difficult to see this experience, lauded time and again as a defining modern phenomenon, as anything but an intellectual descendant of the ancient monks' angst-ridden boredom in the desert.

Camus' strange and zombie-like character Meursault is an archetypal inheritor of this tradition. He senses that the physical world as a whole is indifferent to his existence and instinctively responds when he refuses to conform to society's expectations. Meursault will not conform for the puzzled world's sake, and his curious honesty – his refusal to feign grief over his mother's death, or guilt over the murder he commits, or attachment to his friends and avocation – is often held up as a commendable product of this existential malaise. It's no surprise that Meursault also rejects any belief in traditional religious systems. Nevertheless, he is an exemplary if unappealing modern manifestation of the acedia that the Christian Evagrius describes.

Acedia is more than just indifference or apathy. Jennifer Radden, in *The Nature of Melancholy*, argues that acedia is 'a distinct category, capturing a state that arose with the unique cultural conditions associated with the desert fathers', and Madeleine Bouchez sees it as 'ennui belonging to the cloister'. But acedia, in various forms, spread far beyond the unique conditions of the desert. The American writer and poet Andrew Solomon entitled his autobiographical encounter with depression *The Noonday Demon* (2001). Kathleen Norris, an intriguing poet, goes one step further in *Acedia & Me* and links the condition both to depression and boredom. 'Is acedia depression?' she asks, and replies, 'Not exactly.'

Why? Because it is an 'oppressive boredom . . . lodged firmly within us'.

At the heart of Evagrius' acedia is chronic boredom. Evagrius himself, in his description of the condition, stresses the desire of the hermit for escape, the predictability of his life, his disgust with it, and his perception of the slowing of time. Demons have nothing to do with what afflicts Evagrius' hermits, nor, as some might suggest, does lack of faith or willpower. Any experience that is repetitious, long lasting, predictable, confining, inescapable, that slows time's passing and that is often distasteful to its sufferer, is bound to produce boredom. In his *Boredom and the Religious Imagination* Michael Raposa suggests that 'we typically associate boredom with the landscape of the desert, with flatness, dryness'. The hermits faced that landscape, stretching off into infinity, on a daily basis. Evagrius' Desert of Cells was well named. Grimy confinement and predictability, not the supernatural, crafted these monks' prototypical version of existential boredom. Boredom, of the simple variety, is at the root.

The appearance of acedia on an altogether more temperate continent makes this connection clearer. In the French monastic communities of John Cassian (c. 370–435 CE), confinement was much less severe. Cassian, the first to bring the monasticism of the deserts to the West, founded two monasteries at the tomb Abbey of St Victor in Marseilles in 415. In France the ascetic individualism of the North African hermit was tempered by the solace of an orderly religious community and by a milder sky. Confinement was diminished. The lower levels of frustration that were the result of Cassian's collective world seem to have mitigated the demonic aspects of Evagrius' bleakly individualist version of acedia. Cassian did include acedia in his famous list of vices, but acedia is for him above all laziness and inertia, an indifference and apathy and, as a result, an unwillingness to pursue spiritual exercises. It's a desire to escape the present, a tiredness, and a hunger for variety. Acedia is characterized by the slowing of time and by a desire to escape the confinement of the monastic routine through sleep or company. This psychological state is not the condition described by Evagrius. In the tenth book of his *Institutes*, in a chapter entitled 'On the Spirit of Acedia', Cassian shows how

> Our sixth combat is with what the Greeks call *acedia*, which we may term weariness or distress of heart. This is similar to dejection, and is especially trying to hermits, and a dangerous and frequent enemy of those who dwell in the desert. It is especially disturbing for a monk at about the sixth hour [noon]. It is like some fever which seizes him at set times and which brings the burning heat of its attacks on the sick man at usual and regular intervals.

The demon is still there, but his power is diminished. The condition of acedia, compared here to a recurrent fever, has been instead 'medicalized' or even pathologized. It has moved inside the sufferer, as a gloomy 'weariness or distress of heart' or 'dejection' rather than demonic interference from without. Cassian goes on to say that the danger of this strange condition is that it will cause the monk (and he is speaking of monks rather than hermits) to abandon his religious vocation and, as a result, to despair of the goodwill of God. Cassian's remedy is for the monks to busy themselves. That is the oldest of all cures for simple boredom.

Cassian places great stress on the wilful laziness that he sees as a key element of the vice of acedia. The condition is more the result of personal weakness than of an inability to resist the onslaught of any devil. That ascetics and hermits such as Evagrius named their boredom as a demon shows how confused and tormented they were: for them, boredom was exacerbated by the extreme solitude and deprivation of their harsh and grimy lives. The early Church, lacking the medical textbooks that might have diagnosed their malady properly, didn't have a clue what it was dealing with. The desire to contain and to classify the uncontrollable and the un-nameable led to its being called a sin, and thence acedia. By contrast, in John Cassian's community the monks lived together, worked together, ate together and prayed together on a daily basis. Gone were the heat, the bad food and water, the snakes and the scorpions, and the relentless solitude and confinement of the desert. Acedia changed with this new world. In this easier monastic life the more virulent acedia of Evagrius is replaced by laziness and an easy boredom.

Looking back over these two exemplars of the tradition of acedia, it's not hard to see why the emotion of acedia became a vice that was demonized or lumped in with psychosis and became pathologized. This was because of the quite reasonable fear that it could lead to a doubting of the goodwill of God. For this reason it became an object of fear and opprobrium. By rendering it thus, acedia becomes easier to understand and to control. What was at root perhaps no more than the simple physical reaction to the unrelenting confinement of boredom came to take on existential and even romantic significance. The early Church fathers over-intellectualized the emotion for the simple reason that it was disruptive and damaging of the religious control required of a person if he were to live successfully as a hermit or a monk. Evagrius does this by blaming a demon and Cassian by confusing it with spiritual boredom and sloth. But the demon conveniently stayed on.

Christian acedia represents the starting point for the Western tradition and for conceptualization of the condition of existential boredom. Calling boredom 'acedia' instilled a sense of its import to potential spiritual renegades in the early Christian Church. In subsequent centuries, calling boredom by other over-dignified names – *mal de vivre*, ennui, or 'inner' or 'spiritual' or 'existential' boredom – has simply become self-important.

The monks' understanding of acedia comes down to the Renaissance period as melancholia. Both conditions, acedia and melancholia, are often conflated by cultural historians with modern existential boredom. In the Renaissance the responsibility for this version of existential boredom begins to shift from the demonic, and from sin, to medicine. In some ways the shift reflects that which can be observed between Evagrius and Cassian. The illness moves inside a person and, so it follows, it comes to belong to medicine more than to theology. But the biblical origins of this bookish condition are never effaced.

Melancholia is a Greek medical term meaning black bile. It has no spiritual overtones at all. Nor did it ever acquire any. In the ancient Greek school of Hippocratic medicine melancholia is one of the four humours within humans that are necessary for good health – phlegm, yellow bile and blood are the others. Hippocratic medicine derives from the fifth and fourth centuries BCE and its extant writing purports to be the work of the school's founder, Hippocrates (born *c.* 460 BCE). This enormously influential medical creed was later made canonical by the ancient physician and philosopher Galen (129–*c.* 200 CE) whose teaching held sway until the seventeenth century and the discoveries of William Harvey. According to the Hippocratic school and to Galen, too much black bile meant that a person would fall prey to melancholia; depression in our terms. Good health in this ancient medical system, which ruled the roost for over a millennium, required a balance between the four humours.

There are many testaments to the Renaissance condition of melancholia. Burton's *Anatomy of Melancholy* and *Hamlet* are the two most famous. In Burton's case, however, melancholia is of a very specific variety: it is the product of excessive scholarly cerebration. There are striking instances of this tradition in the visual art of the period. One is the copperplate engraving by Albrecht Dürer (1471–1528), *Melencolia I* (1514) and another is a reaction against this, a painting entitled *Melancholia* (1532) by his contemporary, Lucas Cranach the Elder (1472–1553). In both works, melancholia is personified as an angel. That the angel represents melancholia is clear from the accoutrements by which she is surrounded, and from the posture she has adopted as well as from the titles of the paintings themselves.

19 Albrecht Dürer, *Melencolia I*, 1514

Dürer's angel looks bored with life on earth and homesick for the celestial realms, but there is a much less obvious, though more important reason for her glumness. Her melancholy is the product of her overactive intellectual life. Dürer's thought was in line with a number of other exemplars of this tradition. (Robert

Burton's *Anatomy of Melancholy* is another.) But the link between too much thinking and melancholy is much older than Dürer, Burton and the Renaissance. Its most famous proponent was the Greek physician Rufus of Ephesus, who was active in the second century of our era, and who highlighted the psychological dangers of the geometrical, architectural and mathematical sciences – precisely the intellectual pursuits which Dürer's angel seems to be pondering excessively. On the floor (next to the sphere, a symbol of the melancholy planet, Saturn), is a variety of implements of the geometer's or architect's trade: a paring chisel, a plane, a pair of pliers half hidden beneath the angel's dress, a saw, a ruler, four nails, and some sort of blowing device. There are more in the centre of the engraving: a brazier with a pot, or athanor, boiling upon it, a pair of tongs, partly obscured, presumably for using with the brazier, a hammer, a polyhedron, an inkpot and a partly obscured plume. The angel of melancholy is holding a geometer's compass in her right hand and rests her right forearm on a book, caught in the act of thought. Thinking, particularly as it relates to geometry and architecture, has caused an excess of black bile within the angel's unfortunate constitution. The intellectual causes of her Renaissance version of existential boredom surround her.

Although Albrecht Dürer's angel is melancholic – in our parlance, depressive – she is also quite clearly angry. Look at her eyes: these are the least angelic orbs that it is possible to imagine. It's easy to miss this, for the fury in those eyes is belied by her languid, tired body. Her posture (elbow planted on knee, hand supporting drooping head) may seem to be a textbook image of a bored person, but her fist is clenched rather than cupping her cheek. At any moment, you feel, this angel could leap up and act out that barely suppressed passion. Angels are not supposed to be that angry. But this angelic anger links back to Evagrius' portrait of acedia. For Evagrius' hermit, religious solitude seemed to breed anger. Continual confinement and predictability meant his boredom cycled into anger, agitation and mania. Dürer's angel may be frustrated with the boredom inherent in an intellectual life as solitary and frustrating as the anchoritic life was for Evagrius' monks. Perhaps her anger even represents a rejection of this boring but divinely ordained mode of being. This might be put in a more familiar manner. The angel's anger may represent a possible rejection of the beneficence of God, which was of course the very behaviour that so concerned Evagrius and Cassian. The condition of existential boredom is typified by a breakdown in the relationship between the individual and the world about him. What is being dealt with here is something of the same order. For the angel the world is God: does her passionate demeanour suggest that she is questioning that world?

The influence that Dürer has had on the vision of the scholar-intellectual as a victim of melancholia – or existential boredom – is fascinating. That the scholar's life can be a very boring one I can confirm from experience. Beginnings, endings, discoveries are exciting, but the drudgery of archival research, in all its forms, and the tedium of writing are not to be underestimated. But scholars dislike to admit this. They tend to dignify their proneness to simple boredom by inventing intellectually impressive terms for it. Scholars can suffer from acedia, or existential boredom, or even melancholia, but they are never bored or depressed by their work.

Scholars, let it be said, are especially prone to melancholia. This is what they believe. It often causes them to expire in the midst of their research and sometimes even to hang themselves in their studies. The great Renaissance scholar Burton survived the illness for most of his life. He kept it at bay by writing his enormous *Anatomy of Melancholy*. But it got him in the end, despite his amusing dismissal of his own kind: 'your greatest students are commonly . . . silly soft fellows in their outward behaviour, absurd, ridiculous to others . . . Are these men not fools?' Rufus of Ephesus understood this form of depression too: 'I know a person in whom melancholy began . . . This man was gentle, and the sadness and fear which afflicted him were not strong . . . The reason for his illness was the constant contemplation of geometrical sciences.' The tradition extends down through Mr Edward Casaubon in George Eliot's *Middlemarch* (1871–1872):

> For my part I am very sorry for him. It is an uneasy lot at best, to be what we call highly taught and yet not to enjoy: to be present at this great spectacle of life and never to be liberated from a small hungry shivering self – never to be fully possessed by the glory we behold, never to have our consciousness rapturously transformed into the vividness of thought, the ardour of a passion, the energy of an action, but always to be scholarly and uninspired, ambitious and timid, scrupulous and dim-sighted.

Casaubon lives on in Jørgen Tesman, the husband of Hedda Gabler, and as Peter Kien in the drear pages of Elias Canetti's *Auto da Fé* (1935). The late W.G. Sebald in his clever, but enormously boring novel, *The Rings of Saturn* (1995), gives more evidence for this strange phenomenon of conjoined depression and scholarly thought. In it, a couple of Romance language lecturers in Norwich literally succumb to this illness of melancholy – and die. One of them, Janine Dakyns, is described as a Flaubert expert who 'sitting there amidst her papers . . . resembled the angel in Dürer's *Melancholia*, steadfast among the instruments of destruction'. The instruments of destruction are not those of the angel, but Janine Dakyns' own boring and unmanageable scholarly papers. The angel might perhaps have not disagreed.

Orhan Pamuk's autobiographical *Istanbul* (2003) also has melancholy as its central motif. This magnificent book is perhaps the most extensive and powerful literary evocation of melancholy linked to too much thinking – yet another variant of existential boredom. Melancholy, or its related Turkish term, *hüzün* ('which denotes a melancholy that is communal rather than private', Pamuk points out), occurs at least once on every second page of the 2004 English translation. The nearest rivals in frequency to this term, though these are far less common, are, unsurprisingly, boredom and nostalgia. Although Pamuk does not connect his version of melancholy and *hüzün* (a 'black passion') with Dürer's angel and her black bile, he does liken his evocation of this emotion three times to that of Robert Burton. And, of course, the narrator of *Istanbul* is a highly intellectual individual, quite a scholar, and enrolled as an architecture student in Istanbul by the end of the novel. Although as subject to *hüzün* as all of the rest of Istanbul, his family are noteworthy for their skill in mathematics and engineering. He and his family have the same interests as Albrecht Dürer's angel. Maybe the melancholy-ridden cityscape of Pamuk's *Istanbul* has a bizarre parallel in the melancholy landscape of Dürer's *Melencolia I*. Perhaps both in fact represent the cityscape of boredom.

Lucas Cranach the Elder was a near contemporary of Albrecht Dürer. They are said to have met in 1508. Cranach's various depictions of melancholia, however, are bound together by his rejection of the secularizing tendencies of Dürer. Cranach's melancholia paintings seem to look back to something akin to a noonday demon as the cause of the emotional state that they evoke.

20 Lucas Cranach the Elder, *Melancholia*, 1532

Composed eighteen years after Dürer's engraving, Cranach's *Melancholia* is deeply, but paradoxically, indebted to *Melencolia I*. It shares some elements: the tools, the sphere as the symbol of Saturn, patron deity of melancholy, the sleeping dog, and the putti. But the differences are marked, visually and conceptually. With her benign, almost bland expression, Cranach's angel is the very antithesis of Dürer's alarmingly angry figure. She is whittling rather than writhing with the life of the mind. And Cranach's background landscape is also less alarming. It comprises, in the main, browned-off winter forests – winter is the time of year traditionally associated with melancholia. The putti are having more fun in Cranach's version than the solitary putto in *Melencolia I*. The birds are new and Cranach's dog looks much more content than that of Dürer. Perhaps the strongest difference between the two representations is in the cloud in the top left of Cranach's painting. It contains images of demonic possession, which may point to the influence of Lucas Cranach's friend, Martin Luther. Plagues and misfortunes generally, believed Luther, are the work of the devil. The approaching cloud perhaps resembles a sort of noonday demon. Here, then, is the nub of Cranach's simple and un-intellectualized understanding of melancholy: the illness – existential boredom or melancholia – is the work of the devil, just as it was for Evagrius.

What Cranach does share with Dürer is this: melancholy, like acedia, involves the rejection or the misperception of the beneficence of the Creator. Where they seem to differ is in their aetiology for the state. For Albrecht Dürer the problem is the deleterious effect of the life of the mind. For Lucas

Cranach the Elder it is the persistent work of the devil, a noonday demon. But in both cases the situational cause – whether scholarly or spiritual – is also linked to something physical in the body, the black bile, whose contemporary importance neither Dürer nor Cranach can quite avoid.

* * *

One of the most famous of all over-thoughtful intellectuals was a 32-year-old schoolteacher from Le Havre. This short, half-blind, ugly young man, who frequently had a large red pimple on his nose and who appears to have had no taste for his own company, was a would-be tomcat and a future philosopher. He disliked school teaching just as much as he disliked being trapped in the French provinces. He was a long way from Paris, and he was even further from John Cassian's rackety city of Marseilles where his alter ego, Antoine Roquentin, fetched up after six years in Indo-China and the East. But this school-teacher did write a very great novel that continues the tradition of the acedia of Evagrius, of Cassian and, of course, that continues the tradition of the melancholia of Dürer. This Frenchman will depict an acedia or a melancholia, or what most critics would term an existential boredom, that results not from despair in the beneficence of the Creator, but from despair in the beneficence of the universe.

The passage to follow comes from a book that the existentialist philosopher Jean-Paul Sartre had intended to call *Melancholia*. Through the original title, reports his biographer Annie Cohen-Solal, Sartre aimed to make clear the link between his own work and Albrecht Dürer's engraving and, as well, the whole classical tradition of melancholia. Sartre's novel was accepted on its second submission, by the Paris publisher Gaston Gallimard, in 1938 and had its title changed, by editorial fiat, to *Nausea*. The quotation to follow concerns what Jean-Paul Sartre terms 'contingency' – his version of melancholia. It describes how the novel's 30-year-old protagonist, the morose Antoine Roquentin, comes to understand that existence is accidental (contingent, what else?) and that there is no necessary connection between an individual and the world around. Roquentin's insight, a linear descendant of the monk's acedia and the ninetieth psalm, is that the universe ('reality') is not just lacking in beneficence, but it is also completely indifferent to the lives of modern anchorites such as himself:

This moment was extraordinary. I was there, motionless and icy, but something fresh had just appeared in the very heart of this ecstasy; I understood the Nausea, I possessed it. To tell the truth, I did not formulate my discoveries to myself. But I think it would be easy for me to put them into words now. The essential thing is contingency. I mean that one cannot define existence as necessity. To exist is simply *to be there*; those who exist let themselves be encountered, but you can never deduce anything from them. I believe there are people who have understood this. Only they tried to overcome this contingency by inventing a necessary, causal being. But no necessary being can explain existence: contingency is not a delusion, a probability which can be dissipated; it is the absolute, consequently the perfect free gift. All is free, this park, this city and myself. When you realize this, it turns your heart upside down and everything begins to float . . .

Sartre tries to show that reality is completely and unexpectedly foreign to the viewer. This motif occurs regularly in the book: a doorknob can seem strange and unknown, as can a seat, or the narrator's own hands. At one point Roquentin's body seems so alien to him that he wants to stab himself to prove that it actually is his – not that this would have proved anything, because shortly afterwards he is certain that he is a crab. No wonder that even sexual intercourse seems to hold little allure for this cancroid historian and for his equally contingent ex-girlfriend, Anny: the pleasure is all somebody else's. And, not long after the crab episode, the apathetic Roquentin discovers, as might have been expected, that 'things are divorced from their names' and that the condition he suffers is 'no longer an illness or a passing fit: it is I'.

The 'illness' that Roquentin endured before reaching this state of enlightenment is a strong sense of disgust which he calls 'Nausea' or 'the filth'. The malaise usually occurs when Roquentin begins to understand that there is no possibility of describing 'existence as necessity'. Sartre registers contingency in vivid terms of disgust. We've already seen how different terms for nausea and biliousness are often adopted as synonyms for simple boredom, and that disgust and simple boredom both keep people clear of toxins (actual and social). So, whereas the small child is often 'fed up' when bored, the grown-up French philosopher suffers Nausea. The genial but acerbic William Ian Miller, in his book *The Anatomy of Disgust*, catches this when he describes these Sartrean forms of existential boredom as a 'generalized "nausea" [and as] a kind of self-congratulatory self-disgust'.

The following is the description of a bout of 'the filth'. It happens just as Antoine is about to enter the café, the Railwaymen's Rendezvous, to have sex with its proprietress, Françoise. He settles for a beer instead. Françoise was elsewhere.

> I felt my shirt rubbing against my chest and I was surrounded, seized by a slow coloured mist, and a whirlpool of lights in the smoke, in the mirrors, in the booths glowing at the back of the café, and I couldn't see why it was there or why it was like that. I was on the doorstep, I hesitated to go in and then there was a whirlpool, an eddy, a shadow passed across the ceiling and I felt myself pushed forward. I floated, dazed by luminous fogs dragging me in all directions at once. Madeleine came floating over to take off my overcoat and I noticed she had her hair drawn back and had on earrings: I did not recognize her. I looked at her large cheeks which never stopped rushing towards the ears. In the hollow of her cheeks, beneath the cheekbones, there were two pink stains which seemed weary on this poor flesh. The cheeks ran, ran towards the ears . . .

As hallucinatory passages like these illustrate, the 'filth' loosens the connections between the self, the world, and meaning. This is the very danger that the early Christian anchorites perceived in acedia. For Evagrius and John Cassian all of creation reflects the beneficent design of God and for these Christians there is a clear and causal link between the Creator, creation and its creatures. Acedia brought its victim to doubt that link. For Roquentin, of course, it's that very link that is in doubt – and he reviles those who have 'tried to overcome this contingency by inventing a necessary, causal being'. If John Cassian could have risen from the dead and had met Antoine on his arrival in Marseilles I am sure he would have diagnosed him straight away as a sufferer of acedia.

A number of situations and images link Roquentin's Nausea and his sense of contingency with monastic acedia. These also make clear the utter boredom of Antoine's life. He may not use the term, but Sartre's descriptions are suffused with a sense of the emotion. The boredom cycles into depression – or melancholy, as Sartre puts it. Roquentin states that 'I live alone, entirely alone. I never speak to anyone, never'. Except for sex with Françoise at the Railwaymen's Rendezvous it is a silent life of monastic solitude. He speaks too of a 'dryness of perception' and of a sadness and exhaustion which mirror remarkably the complaints in the scribal work of the later monastics who became subject to acedia. Roquentin writes, in the most sour of ways, 'work today – I wrote six pages'. Like Rufus of Ephesus' scholars or Dürer's angel, Antoine Roquentin has thought himself into a state of melancholy. He seems to find the life of a historian and writer a very boring one indeed and within this emaciated life Roquentin has come to doubt not the beneficence of God, the cause of the monastic acedia, but the beneficence of the universe. So he'll say, 'I exist, that's all. And that trouble is so vague, so metaphysical that I am ashamed of it.'

Sartre derives his conception of contingency from the enormously influential German philosopher Martin Heidegger. Sartre spent some time in Berlin (bored for quite a bit of the stay) on a French government scholarship just before the Second World War acquainting himself with this thinker. Heidegger's views on boredom provide the direct link between contingency and what we call existential boredom. Heidegger divides boredom more or less into the simple (two forms: where one can be bored by something – a dull piece of music – or with something – too much good food, for example) and the existential. For Heidegger this existential form is experienced when an individual is reduced by circumstances to a state of complete indifference. This is how Antoine Roquentin felt towards his city, acquaintances, his research, sex, his food, and just about everything else with which he came into contact. When a person feels like this, according to Heidegger, they become empty and do not expect, or indeed receive, anything of significance from the world about them. In her article 'Boredom and School' Teresa Belton, an educationalist with an interest in the ideas behind boredom, explains:

Heidegger sees this profound boredom . . . as a 'positive refusal' of the possibilities of doing and acting, as a rejection of responsibility for one's own being. Paradoxically, this condition reveals one as answerable for everything and everyone . . . profound boredom produces the possibility for what he calls 'the moment of vision', 'in which the full situation of an action opens itself and keeps itself open'.

Sartre, in *Nausea,* dramatizes pretty much the same process and in doing so makes it much simpler to understand. The 'vision' is what Roquentin terms contingency, the proper understanding of the relationship between the individual and the world around.

There is a very long religious and biblical tradition behind Sartre's and Heidegger's existential formulations. These formulations, furthermore, link squarely with the emotion of disgust. The denomination of existential boredom as nausea is not Sartre's invention. Its basis is of course physiological, for boredom stands in close relation to disgust, and disgust leads very easily to nausea and to biliousness. But existential boredom seems to have intellectualized this basic emotional response and in so doing to have disguised its origins.

Nausea, as a symptom of boredom, appears in a variety of unexpected contexts from the ancient world to today. The asthmatic and vastly wealthy Roman statesman and philosopher Seneca (*c.* 4 BCE–65 CE), acted as an advisor to the notorious emperor Nero between 54 and 62 CE. His was a role that was steeped in compromise and corruption – hence his visceral understanding of emotional ambivalence. Seneca understands boredom as seasickness, and uses the Greek term *nausia* in a very famous passage in his *Epistles* 24.26. No doubt Sartre knew this gobbet from his years at the elite Parisian secondary school, the Lycée Louis le Grand:

'How long will things be the same? Surely I will be awake, I will sleep, I will be hungry, I will be cold, I will be hot. Is

there no end? Do all things go in a circle? . . . Night over-
comes day, day night, summer gives way to autumn, winter
presses on autumn which is checked by spring. All things
pass that they may return. I do nothing new, I see nothing
new. Sometimes this makes me seasick/nauseous.' There
are many who judge living not painful but empty.

Seneca's pessimism is experienced in the gizzard. There is the
yawning, the sameness of things, the infinite repetition of
events. It all makes him disgusted, and that disgust is registered
as a type of nausea or seasickness. It's almost as if Seneca had
said, simply, that 'this makes me sick': we would have understood immediately that he was bored. Seneca's boredom,
which he glosses as seasickness, may not match Sartre's philosophical Nausea. But it offers him a useful term.

Seneca was not alone in linking boredom and seasickness.
The Roman poet Horace (65–68 BCE) speaks of simple
boredom in his *Epistles* 1.1.92–93: 'when [the poor man] has
rented a boat,' Horace writes, 'he gets as seasick [*nauseat*] as
the rich man whom a private trireme conveys.' What Horace
means is that the rich and the poor become equally bored by
extravagance – the only difference is the scale. Seneca's
language is also picked up in a remarkable passage by Plutarch
in his *Life of Pyrrhus* 13. Of the Macedonian regent Pyrrhus
(319–272 BCE) Plutarch says that 'he thought not offering ill
to others and not receiving it from others was a sort of
nauseous boredom (*alus nautiodes* "seasick-like boredom")'.
Pyrrhus had by this time given up his life of conquest and he
was totally bored by his retirement. It's interesting that

Plutarch pulls the Greek terms for nausea (seasickness) and boredom (*alus*) together in this sentence. The link that Plutarch recognized fed directly into the tradition of existential boredom. But Pyrrhus' problem was not existential, but simple.

By the eighteenth and nineteenth centuries nausea had been thoroughly intellectualized and 'existentialized', though its linguistic debt to the simple version of antiquity is apparent. Immanuel Kant (1724–1804) believed humans feel a nausea at their own existence (which is boring). Flaubert in his letters to Louise Colet speaks of the 'nausea of ennui' – a phrase extremely close to Plutarch's *alus nautiodes*. The one-time classical scholar Friedrich Nietzsche would have known of the tradition of Senecan nausea. The emotion figures regularly in his work, in the *Genealogy of Morals* (1887), for example, and above all in *Thus Spoke Zarathustra* (1883–1885) where the 'great nausea' and the 'great pity' are central motifs. Nausea (estrangement from the human world) is one of the challenges which Zarathustra must overcome. Here it represents estrangement much as it did for Evagrius.

Nausea's etymological roots, and its connection with boredom of the simple variety, is wonderfully figured by the American artist Edward Hopper (1882–1967) in his painting *Rooms by the Sea* (1951). Working around fourteen years after the publication of *Nausea*, the gangly, reclusive, monogamous Hopper may not have known of Sartre's writing, let alone of Seneca. But he had spent time in Paris as a younger man more than once, and he certainly knew very well the poetry of Baudelaire, with its concern with ennui and its disdain for the bourgeoisie. I am sure that Jean-Paul Sartre's notorious dislike of middle-class domesticity finds an echo in *Rooms by the Sea*.

The nausea in this painting comes from that unexpected drop from the front door into the ocean, which creates an awful feeling of vertigo. It is Sartre's contingency in a visual form: the dizzying instability of this world that contains Hopper's living room and the *alus nautiôdês* of the ocean. The bilious green colours of the carpets, too, match the way the sea outside the front door makes the viewer feel. (I am sure that if boredom has a colour, then it must be linked to nausea – to whatever colours can be joined with visceral disgust: green, orangey brown, and colours often associated with illness and

21 Edward Hopper, *Rooms by the Sea*, 1951

vomiting.) And a number of other motifs of boredom clamour for attention in this eerily still painting.

Rooms by the Sea is something of an archetype of visual depictions of boredom. What many paintings have in common, in terms of composition, is the use of flat space and strong, ordered lines (planes, panels and frames and so forth) contrasting with an extensive, infinite vista outside the confining area. (Where the representation is more fluid and chaotic, where space avoids the linear and begins to swirl, more often than not depression or melancholy is the subject.) Hopper's painting has these tenets of boredom in spades. The glimpse of the horizon points to the theme of infinity, the open door leading to that 'endless monotony' (in Oblomov's words) of the sea itself. The only sense of movement or change is the predictable rippling of the sea's surface – there is nothing happening in the house, except perhaps (as I like to imagine) the older man and the young woman from Walter Sickert's *Ennui* seated just around the corner in the living room. Hopper's characteristic use of flattened planes of light and clear lines emphasizes the sense of containment and tedium. The choice seems to be between the stifling claustrophobia of the middle-class living room, or the vertiginous expanse of the ocean. Perhaps Hopper was saying something about middle-class American life in the 1950s – that in his eyes it was drowningly boring.

* * *

What is existential boredom? I don't believe that this brief survey has made an answer any easier to formulate. There are many similarities between acedia, melancholia, Nausea, and the tradition of seasickness. Are they sufficient for us to say, yes, *here* is existential boredom? Or, rather, is the concept such a broad one, so general in its application, so umbrella-like in its inclusiveness, that it becomes a chimera? My opinion is that this is so. There may be too many dissimilarities between acedia, melancholia and Nausea for them to have clear ties within lived experience. I suspect that this tradition is more the product of the intellect.

Be that as it may, it's widely accepted that existential boredom – because it's associated with a fundamental despair in the bene- ficence of God or the universe – can threaten one's very exis- tence. This is such an important theme relating to boredom that it can't be passed over. Let's begin with the nuttiest of all links: that between boredom and death, which in its strange way is typical of this doleful tradition. The case for simple boredom's ability to kill was made in a commentary published in April 2010 in the *International Journal of Epidemiology* by Annie Britton and Martin Shipley of University College London, which maintained that it's possible that the more (simply) bored you are, the more likely you are to die at a younger age. These two psychologists examined questionnaires filled out between 1985 and 1988 by more than 7,500 London civil servants between the ages of 35 and 55. These workers had been asked if they had felt bored at work during the previous month. By ascertaining how many respondents had died by April 2009 the psychologists discovered that 'those who reported they had been very bored were two and a half times more likely to die of a heart problem than those who hadn't reported being bored'. It is comforting to learn that Britton and Shipley said boredom was probably not in itself that deadly. Rather, 'the state of boredom is almost certainly a proxy for other risk factors', they reported. 'It is likely that those who were bored were also in poor health.' This is just as well. Otherwise I'd have been dead many years ago.

Research like this seems to draw its legitimacy from the very common causal association between existential boredom and death. It is often asserted that the experience of boredom can become so powerful as to drive an individual to suicide. Because it's associated with a despair in the beneficence of the God or of the universe, it easily seems to lead to suicide. If God or the universe don't care, then what point is there in life? When Seneca says 'there are many who judge living not painful but empty' he sets the stage. And Seneca ended up knowing a lot about suicide. It's how his own life ended. Sartre regularly picks up the theme of suicide in *Nausea*. One of Roquentin's insights is that 'I have no right to live' or, as he puts it elsewhere, 'I am free: there is absolutely no more reason for living'. In Orhan Pamuk's *Istanbul*, suicide is a persistent motif that is jumbled up with melancholy, boredom, nostalgia and loneliness. Then there are those venerable Church Fathers with whom this chapter began. Evagrius describes his North Africa hermit as being so harried by the noonday demon, it 'makes him dislike his place . . . [and] his life itself'.

The victims of existential boredom should have been dropping like flies. But in fact they were not. The link between boredom and suicide seems stronger in literary texts than in real life. Once again intellect displaces lived experience. So it is that the British novelist Graham Greene claimed in his writings that as a young man he was so deeply bored with life that he used to play Russian roulette, just to spice things up. He died of old age. Suicide might be more common amongst creative individuals, but artists perish, as the psychologist Kay Redfield Jamison explains, because they are ill, not because they are existentially bored. And Emma Bovary? She might have launched her affairs because she was bored, but she killed herself because she'd been disgraced. Victims of existential boredom – but not simple boredom – may talk a lot about suicide. But if they do anything about killing themselves it's usually on paper.

It's in dramatic or in fictional tales that romantic suicides are most frequently to be found. They are usually cast in the narrative mould of 'resistance and self-affirmation' in the face of an existential crisis. Choice may have been removed by the hostility or indifference of society, or of the universe, or even of God, but the alienated individual may resist and affirm through the exercise of free choice as it is expressed in the decision to end one's own life. Hedda Gabler, for instance, offers a classic example of the strong-minded individual who has become trapped in a tedious position where free choice in lifestyle is no longer an option. Henrik Ibsen's play, dating from 1890, offers one of the most puzzling portrayals of the apparent mortal danger of boredom and depicts a heroine who strikes back at existential boredom by taking her own life.

The play is set wholly in a house in Oslo (then Christiania). It's Hedda Gabler's new home. Hedda, the aristocratic daughter of a general, is just back from her honeymoon with Jørgen Tesman, an aspiring but not especially brilliant young academic. Early on in the play, Hedda makes clear to the sinister Judge Brack just how boring she finds her new life and her marriage.

HEDDA: Uh – the rooms all seem to smell of lavender and dried rose-leaves. – But perhaps it's Aunt Julia that has brought that scent with her.

BRACK: [*Laughing.*] No, I think it must be a legacy from the late Mrs. Secretary Falk.

HEDDA: Yes, there is an odour of mortality about it. It reminds me of a bouquet – the day after the ball. [*Clasps her hands behind her head, leans back in her chair and looks at him.*] Oh, my dear Judge – you cannot imagine how horribly I shall bore myself here.

It is a very bleak exchange.

When Hedda's husband looks set to be pipped for a university position by her old lover, the alcoholic Ejlert Løvborg, it seems that their straitened finances will mean Hedda having to give up the regular entertaining and the extravagant housekeeping she had in mind. She'll have to look domestic boredom very hard in the visage. Hedda, through a series of accidents, manages to encourage Løvborg to do away with himself. She even gives him a pistol, urging him to resist and affirm with a 'beautiful death'. He should put a bullet in his heart. Løvborg almost accepts her suggestion. Hedda subsequently learns from the concupiscent Judge Brack that Ejlert's death occurred by accident, in a brothel, and by a misfired shot in the bowel. It's good news for Brack. It gives him power over Hedda Gabler. Her response? She leaves the room and shoots herself in the temple.

Why did Hedda kill herself? To carry through the 'beautiful' death that Løvborg should have achieved? To escape the lubricious designs of Judge Brack? Out of guilt because she'd caused Løvborg's death? Or did she commit suicide to avoid the dreary boredom of humdrum life with her dull scholar husband, unenlivened by parties and pretty things? Perhaps for all of these reasons. But Hedda Gabler's death has often been understood as a sublime act motivated by existential boredom. She resists the boring Jørgen Tesman, resists the boring aunt, Julianne Tesman, resists boring home life, resists Løvborg's boring compromise, resists the sleazy Judge Brack and, through all of this, she affirms her personal and spiritual independence and rejects boring compromise by killing herself.

In real life, of course, Hedda could have said no at any point to any of the misfortunes that befell her. In real life this is just what she'd have done. She wouldn't have burnt Løvborg's manuscript. She would not have put herself in Judge Brack's debt. And above all, she would not have killed herself. She would have endured, just as all of us do when we are bored and compromised.

Suicide has no clear relationship with boredom. Suicide, especially, has nothing necessarily to do with the bookish existential boredom. There is no death-producing pain involved in an intellectual perception of the meaninglessness of life, unless that perception is the product of painful depression. To link boredom, simple or existential, with suicide is a belittling exercise. Suicide is the product of racking psychological pain. It is trivialized when it is used as a symbol for boredom. Hedda's unfortunate death, typical of so many other literary suicides, does nothing but demean. It's as if her and others' existential boredom becomes a strikingly more important condition if it can be seen to provoke its sufferers into taking their own lives, rather than leaving them smelly, solitary, and rather insufferable.

* * *

The topic of existential boredom is a huge one. Many learned volumes have been written on the subject. I've just touched a tiny tip of a mighty iceberg in this chapter. But what I hope to have shown is how simple boredom becomes caught up and complicated in this bilious and bookish matrix. Sometimes it seems it has been dressed up by those with special interests, such as in religion or philosophy, and has been made to appear something more than it is: thus the bored and depressed hermit suffers acedia; the depressed scholar becomes melancholic; the lonely philosopher becomes the victim of contingency or Nausea. What does fascinate me is that this tradition of existential boredom has a common thread of variations. In its first phase it links the despairing state of the monk described by Evagrius with doubt in the goodwill of God: this produces acedia. In its Renaissance phase, God is displaced by the body: at risk is one's health, and acedia becomes melancholia. In its modern phase acedia shifts into a strange conjunction of depression and a doubt in the goodwill of the world itself.

What does 'existential boredom' mean? The only definition to fully cover it runs as follows: existential boredom entails a powerful and unrelieved sense of emptiness, isolation and disgust in which the individual feels a persistent lack of interest in and difficulty with concentrating on his current circumstances. I wonder if the simplest way to understand existential boredom is not this. It is a concept. It's not an emotion and it's not a feeling. It is a concept that is constructed from a union of boredom, chronic boredom, depression, a sense of superfluity, frustration, surfeit, disgust, indifference, apathy and feelings of entrapment. Above all it's a biblically based concept that has been constructed within a strong intellectual tradition. This much was suggested in an article in the *Guardian* (16 June 2009), when the gifted young British writer, Lee Rourke listed his 'top ten books about boredom'. Here they are: *William Lovell* (Ludwig Tieck), *Mercier and Camier* (Samuel Beckett), *The Book of Disquiet* (Fernando Pessoa), *Whatever* (Michel Houllebecq), *Melancholy* (Jon Fosse), *Boredom* (Alberto Moravia), *Blue of Noon* (Georges Bataille), *Homo Faber* (Max Frisch), *Hunger* (Knut Hamsun), *Perfect Tense* (Michael Bracewell). Rourke explains that boredom has always fascinated him: 'I suppose it is the Heideggerian sense of "profound boredom" that intrigues me most'. Lee Rourke is speaking of existential boredom, in other words. He is speaking of a condition that, for him, is grounded in a mandarin literary tradition.

I believe that simple boredom also has its own tradition, more fundamentally rooted in human psychology than existential boredom because it is an emotion that has been felt in all periods of history. But this is an assertion that is often denied. Let's see why.

5

Does boredom have a history?

THE ITALIAN CITY OF Benevento, around 50 kilometres north-east of Naples, has a colourful reputation. Today it is famous for its witches (who used to gather there underneath a walnut tree and dance on the Sabbath) and also for the less attractive Camorra. But in antiquity this Campanian city was much tamer. In those days it was called Good Fortune or, in Latin, Beneventum. Despite its promising appellation it was a dull, provincial city. Some of the flavour of the ancient *città* is caught in this inscription, carved in stone and unearthed in the nineteenth century:

> For Tanonius Marcellinus, a most distinguished man of the consular rank and a most worthy patron as well, because of the good deeds by which he rescued the population [of Beneventum] from endless boredom, the entire people [of this city] judges that this inscription should be recorded.

This may be the only public inscription in Western history that praises a public official for rescuing the citizens of his town from boredom (which the *universa plebs* inscribed in the Latin as *taedia* – 'boredom').

I'd like to be able to say something about this remarkable and considerate Tanonius Marcellinus. Unfortunately it is not possible. The inscription says that Tanonius is of consular rank, which means that he was a man of considerable political significance. But his name does not appear in any surviving consular lists, so perhaps the grateful burghers of Beneventum were exaggerating his political status. Who could know? All that can be said with any confidence is that he was graced by this honorific inscription some time in the late third century of our era. He must have been rich if he was able to rescue a whole city from boredom. What the wealthy Tanonius Marcellinus actually did is guesswork, but more likely than not he staged some games in the local amphitheatre; not athletic games, but gladiatorial games which were especially popular with the lower classes of all Roman cities. The administrative echelons used the staging of games as a means of currying the favour of the restless underclasses. If the *universa plebs* in ancient Benevento were restless, it must have been because they were bored. Perhaps the small dry hillside town, cut off from Rome and the momentous events that took place there, and enlivened mostly by market days and trade, presented its poorer citizens with a life of dreary sameness. Perhaps the citizens of Beneventum felt that life was passing them by. Perhaps that's why they were so grateful to Tanonius Marcellinus and his 'good deeds'.

Another Latin wall inscription – a graffito coming from the much more famous Pompeii, inscribed some time in the first century of our era – also records the boredom of the ancients, although this time in a more impish way. The wall is covered in Latin graffiti. Some Roman larrikin has sardonically scratched: 'Wall! I wonder that you haven't fallen down in ruin, when you have to support all the boredom of your inscribers.' Whoever it was that wrote this clearly judged the other inscriptions to be of a pretty poor standard – he found them boring. The wall, nevertheless, 'supports' the existence, two thousand years ago, of a lot of bored people. Just as is the case today, graffiti is often a product of the idle vandalism of bored youth.

To ask whether boredom has a history is to ask two things: first, has boredom always been felt in the same way by humans? And second: has boredom always been a part of human life? The instinctive answer to the first question is that, yes, people have always had the unfortunate capacity to be bored. So, if boredom has always been felt the same way and if the nature of boredom has never changed then, no, it has no history. What's all the fuss about then? Doesn't this inscription honouring Tanonius Marcellinus indicate that? Weren't the plebs of Good Fortune and the unknown Latin graffiti artists bored in just the same way that you and I can be? The answer to the second question, however, clouds the certainty of this easy response. Instinct suggests that, for example, the often dangerous and usually busy life of hunter-gathers, such as the Australian Aboriginals, left less of a temporal margin for boredom than did, say, daily life in ancient Beneventum. So, no, boredom isn't necessarily and at all times part of human life. This is the position that I'd take on boredom. Humans (and many animals) always have had the capacity for this emotion, but not all societies enable or require creatures to experience boredom.

This is not a view that is held by all of the writers who take an interest in boredom. Many argue that boredom was invented in the eighteenth century. They maintain that it became important during the European Enlightenment and in the revolutionary decades that followed. They also believe that the status of boredom was reinforced in the early nineteenth century during the time of the Romantic movement, but that boredom really took off in the twentieth century. According to this group of writers boredom has a very clear and recent history. Their counter-intuitive view has come to dominate the study of boredom. In this chapter I'll try to explain why this has happened. My own opinion, as I have indicated, is that this historicity of boredom is exaggerated. In fact I think that it's the product of a confusion between simple boredom and existential boredom. That's what I find so intriguing about Tanonius Marcellinus of Beneventum. His honorific inscription provides real evidence that we are not alone, historically speaking, when we complain that we are simply bored.

Where does this counter-intuitive view, of the recent invention of boredom, come from? During the last fifty years there has been a lot, interest in the question of whether emotions are subject to contemporary social and economic forces. This form of 'historicism' maintains that each historical epoch has its own ways of feeling, and that individuals are as a result thereby entangled, in terms of their feelings, within their own specific eras: Greeks and Romans, for example, might be expected to have felt the world in a way quite different from us in ours. Adherents to this creed are usually termed 'constructivists'; they believe that humans are walled in, as it were, within the experiential or even knowledge systems of their eras, and that human attitudes and characteristics have been constructed or *invented* in some way or another by the social forces of their particular age. In the opposite corner are the 'essentialists', those who believe that humans are not enclosed within discrete experiential realms, and that there are certain unchangeable essentials in human characters and institutions. They may even believe that there are basic and immutable laws in the area of social behaviour.

It would be wrong to reduce this debate to 'nature and nurture', with the essentialists teamed up under the 'nature' banner and the constructionists gathered in the 'nurture' camp. There's more to it than this simple dichotomy between 'nature or nurture'. I have already discussed the 'cognitive' understanding of emotion – how emotions involve not just *reactions* but at the very same time *evaluations* – and how this has a direct impact on the constructionist understanding of the history of such emotions as boredom. The constructionists believe that the evaluative or cognitive element of emotion is something that is conditioned by the habits of particular societies, languages, and even genders. Take an emotion such as fear. It's been argued that for the Greeks, fear was often a deliberative emotion (sailors in fear for their lives in a storm will weigh the consequences of their actions and carry out their duties with more care). For the Romans, on the other hand, it was often associated with control of others (fear makes a large slave population easier to manage). So, by looking at the way an emotion is registered in different historical eras – at how particular emotions can vary over time, that is to say – we may produce or construct a 'history', a historical narrative of an emotion. That is what I meant by the question: does boredom have a history?

Supporters of this view often attempt to formulate an 'archaeology' of the emotional experiences they study. (The French philosopher Michel Foucault made this term famous in *The Archaeology of Knowledge* [1969].) Such historians attempt to show how there are periods when one or another version of an emotion may predominate, just as the various layers of settlement are exposed at an archaeological dig site. David Konstan, to cite but one exemplar of this approach, is particularly interested in establishing a Greek archaeology. He aims to show how the Greeks understood emotions differently to us.

Curiously, much of the work of the constructionists has led to the conclusion that most of what is popularly thought of as immutably human – parenting habits, for example, or sexual desire, or common emotions such as anger, love and even remorse – is in fact the product of modern times: the European Enlightenment, the Industrial Revolution, or the Romantic movement. The changes that took place then caused the modern human to come into being. As for the essentialists – and there are not so many of them left these days in the social sciences – they will often speak more of 'nature'. Supporters of this view tend to come from the sciences: one of the most notable is the entomologist E.O. Wilson, the inventor of sociobiology, a mode of investigation that looks at social behaviour in animals – how they mate, fight, hunt, swarm and even hive, if they are bees or ants. The sociobiologists argue that just as natural selection leads animals to evolve profitable ways of interacting with the natural environment, so too it led to the genetic evolution of profitable social behaviour. Sociobiologists usually extrapolate their claims concerning animals to humans. To make such a link assumes that practices and behaviours must be universal.

When the question 'does X have a history' is posed, or when the term 'invention' is used, you know that you are liable to be entering constructionist territory. Patricia Meyer Spacks, Elizabeth Goodstein and Yasmine Musharbash, to cite but three of the most interesting writers on boredom, all take a more or less constructionist position on the matter. They present the view that boredom was *invented* and that it derives from the Enlightenment, at its most sophisticated and convincing. By disagreeing with them I may seem to be something of a dog in the manger, but I find it very hard to deny the existence of boredom in archaic Beneventum and on that Pompeian wall. These two pieces of evidence suggest to me that boredom does indeed have a history and that boredom existed long before the Enlightenment.

The belief that boredom was discovered in the eighteenth century during the European Enlightenment is, according to the sociologist Ben Anderson in his article 'Time-stilled space-slowed: how boredom matters', based on 'an intuitive association [of boredom] with the notion of either alienation or anomie'. Boredom, alienation and anomie (so the argument runs) are all uniquely modern phenomena. Until the eighteenth century boredom had remained a marginal experience at best, as it was only in the Age of Reason that the primacy of the individual was put forward. This period challenged theocracy, autocracy, traditional privilege, and the unthinking adherence to a collectivist tradition. It makes sense to attempt to link boredom to a heightened sense of the importance of the individual and of the individual's emotions within this great social change.

Historians with an interest in cultural constructionism usually highlight four or five trends occurring during the Enlightenment which, they believe, were without parallel and which hastened the birth of boredom. They suggest that there was an increased importance given to leisure and a belief in late-modern societies that we have a right to happiness; that there was a decline of Christianity and growth in secularization, which the educationalist Sean Desmond Healy describes as a 'growing metaphysical void at the heart of Western civilization'; that there was a greater concern with individual rights – what Ben Anderson has described as 'the rise of progressive, calculable, individualism'; and finally, an increasing interest in inner experience. Anderson adds a fifth change: bureaucratization. He explains that 'boredom is argued to have emerged in response to the rise of standardized, standardizing, organization of time space'.

Lending even more support to these arguments for boredom's modern appearance is the intriguing claim that the word 'boredom' was not used in English before the eighteenth century. Patricia Meyer Spacks lucidly makes the case for the sudden appearance of the term boredom at this time:

The *Oxford English Dictionary* asserts that the verb *to bore*, as a psychological description, arose 'after 1750' (it does not appear in Johnson's dictionary of 1755). The word can claim no clear etymology, although the dictionary notes and dismisses efforts to connect it with the reiterative action of the bore as a drill and with the French *bourre*, meaning padding. The first occurrence cited comes from a private letter of 1768, Earl Carlisle announcing his pity for 'Newmarket friends, who are to be bored by these Frenchmen.' *Bore*, meaning 'a thing which bores,' comes along in 1778; the bore as tiresome person is assigned to 1812 (although in fact the word in this sense appears several times in the eighteenth century); the first citation of the noun *boredom* belongs to 1864.

Until then, the English-speaking world managed to do without recourse to 'boredom'. If the English were bored before the eighteenth century then presumably they did not know it.

Now, if the changes just highlighted really did take place it's easy to see how they might have caused individuals to begin to suffer from boredom. More leisure provides more opportunity to become bored – that's if leisure time is not well occupied. The decline of Christianity takes away some of the community links that the Church had provided and this meant more alienation. It also removes from individuals the demands of a higher authority, and forces them to decide things for themselves. Individual rights? They were talked of a great deal in the late eighteenth and nineteenth centuries. What of inner experience? Introspection provides the opportunity to realize that you are bored. Bureaucratization? There's probably no greater fuel for alienation and anomie than bundy-punching and inflexible organizations.

And what about the twentieth century? Why is it so important for boredom? It is usually suggested that boredom became more prevalent in this period because of an increase in human isolation, in secularization, and in the loss of human traditions, because of the prevalence of dull work and commercialized leisure and because of a loss of a sense of community. Boredom, if these conditions actually did prevail, has become one of the symptoms of modernity. Many people believe that is the case, and some will even go so far as to describe boredom as another of the villains of modernity. As such, boredom is characterized as a pathological condition. According to Sean Desmond Healy boredom shows an 'intense, desperate, agonized, undirected irritation alternating with sullen, morose, lowering lethargy and an utterly exasperated violence'. And Ben Anderson suggests that 'boredom, once explained, has therefore become a symptom of the "imprint of meaninglessness" . . . in which the nature of matter is dulled. Emerging after rage, but before anxiety, in boredom "one assumes, naturally enough, that all life is empty".'

There really is a puzzle in this material. How can you square the argument that boredom suddenly and relatively recently appeared, and carries such pathological weight, with the historical reality of the inscription of the *universa plebs* of Beneventum? Can the Benevetans have meant something other than boredom by the Latin plural form *taedia*?

Perhaps the answer to this conundrum rests in the word itself. The term 'boredom' connotes two radically different experiences: the simple, and the existential. It appears most likely then that the constructionists and the essentialists are talking about two quite different psychological states, yet using the same word to describe both. When the existence of boredom before the Enlightenment is denied by historians, I suspect what is being denied is the existence of existential boredom before the Enlightenment. I can agree with that. And I am quite sure that they'd be happy to allow any era the capacity to feel simple boredom, although I suspect they might want a new word for the emotion.

The conundrum may go deeper still. You don't have to say *'I'm bored'* to say that you're bored. It seems to me to be quite likely that before the appearance of the term 'boredom' around the time of the Enlightenment people used a variety of different and equally expressive locutions for the emotion. The emergence of the new term 'bored' may reflect nothing other than lexical accident or fashion. In fact there are many ways of saying you're bored in contemporary English, and I am sure this was the case three centuries ago as well. Let me illustrate with a real life encounter.

Last autumn I passed a trinket stall in London near to the entrance of Tate Modern. It was a miserable day. The stalls didn't seem to be doing much business and nor did the tent full of huskies. A sympathetic customer asked a woman running the trinket stall if her work was interesting. The woman smiled and answered: 'It's just a bit tedious. It's just a bit mind-numbing.' She was obviously saying that it was boring (simply, not existentially), but she didn't need to use the obvious adjective.

There are many other colourful circumlocutions and synonyms for boredom that I have encountered. 'He could talk the leg off a chair at fifty paces' is one way to describe a person so dreary that they could 'bore the pants off you'. V.S Pritchett said that a bore has been defined as a man who tells us everything. It would be easier to say that he could yap the leg off an iron pot. A bore is also a pain in the neck or a pain in the arse or even just a pain. A bore can be a drip, a wet blanket, a fish head, a pill, an alf, an oik, or even a bromide. He can make you feel fed up to the gills, or fed up to the back teeth, just plain fed up, wearied, catatonic, or that you've got nothing to do. Or perhaps simply sick. Or even sick to death. Disgusted. Dead behind the eyes. He can kill your time or kill you and he can leave you bored stiff, twiddling your thumbs, jack of him, and reduced to counting nails in a wall, or watching paint dry, or even watching the tap drip. What's boring is blah, bland, never ending, mind numbing, mono-chrome, a drag, QFD (quelle fucking drag), deadly, dull, dreary, soporific, tedious, stale, lifeless, lacklustre, torpid, a torpor, as long as a wet weekend or a month of Sundays. Or just plain flat, insipid, and monotonous or monochrome. Flat as a tack. Dull as ditchwater. Drudgery. Ho hum.

To put the argument into an even clearer perspective, my former student Rhonda Barlow has pointed out to me that for centuries the English language officially lacked a word for something that the English were rather adept at. Astoundingly, the verb 'to defeat' was first used in English in the sixteenth century, meaning 'to unmake', 'to undo' or 'to destroy'. Its specific use for *military* defeat in the modern sense is first attested only in 1562. The *Oxford English Dictionary* cites the meaning of military defeat in the following example: 'J. Shute *Combine's Turk. Wars*: "The armie of Baiazith was defeicted, and taken by Tamerlano".' The use of defeat as a noun, again in the military sense, came later and is first seen in 1600, as follows: 'They had bad newes in Fraunce of the defeat of the armie.' Would anyone wish to deny the English race any concept of the notion of defeating an enemy army on the basis of the relatively late appearance of the verb, in a military context, and the noun 'defeat'? Given the often bloody course of English history, that seems rather unlikely. It is more probable that English-speakers had used a different term, but they still knew what a 'defeat' was. So it is, I suspect, with the term 'boredom', and, as a result, we have to be quite careful about the terminology that is used. Before denying the existence of an emotion in a particular culture, all of the lexical variants used to describe that emotion need to be examined. To my knowledge, the various languages of the Enlightenment have still to be scrutinized for traces of boredom in disguise.

That may be an unnecessary task, of course. As we saw in Chapter 3, an emotion cannot be denied to exist in a human or in animals because they lack the lexical resource to describe that specific emotion. Animals may well experience not just the primary emotions, but also social emotions, amongst which I'd include boredom. If you can accept that argument, it follows that people in any historical era may have the capacity to experience boredom whether or not they have a term for it.

What *may* vary is the degree to which boredom can play a role in human life. It is at this point, I believe, that the broader constructionist position becomes persuasive. A child who lives in a rich and varied environment may rarely experience simple boredom. A child who lives in a less varied environment may, conversely, experience boredom regularly. The same might also be true for animals. And it is likely that this same point could be made for different societies, and for different times. As I suggested at the beginning of this chapter, the often dangerous and usually busy life of hunter-gathers, such as the Australian Aboriginals, may have left less time for boredom than did, say, daily life in ancient Beneventum. Boredom isn't necessarily and at all times part of human life. Humans always have had the capacity for this emotion, I believe, but not all societies enable or require humans to experience boredom. To adapt the terminology of the philosopher John Searle: boredom may be regularly *rediscovered*, rather than *invented*. This notion of rediscovery may offer a more nuanced course between the two hostile extremes of contructivism and essentialism.

Are there cultural exceptions? Are there ever any societies in which boredom is neither expressed directly in its own name nor felt? Patricia Meyer Spacks, of course, can pinpoint the time just before the invention of a name for boredom within the English language: 'Imagining ... the nature of experience before the invention of boredom, I posited a harmonious state in which leisure did not exist as a separate condition, in which focus on community and on spiritual obligation obviated the need for extended introspection, in which people did not worry about the precise degree of happiness and fulfilment in their lives.' It sounds very utopian for little more than 250 years ago.

An outstanding article by the gifted anthropologist Yasmine Musharbash identifies another apparently boredom-less society. Musharbash attributes to pre-colonial Australian Aboriginals 'the ability and willingness "to be in the moment" wherever one is, no matter what happens, "living absolutely in the present"'. 'To be in the moment' meant for them living in a boredom-free world. Aboriginal languages had no word for boredom. Modern-day Australian Aboriginals do experience boredom, Musharbash goes on to point out. Boredom, she believes, arrived with the colonizers, and their imposition of the white civilization's clocks, calendars, lists and linear form of memory upon the native peoples. Colonization divorced the Aboriginals from 'living absolutely in the present', and introduced them to a world of divided time where boredom lurks in its interstices.

What does 'being in the moment' actually mean? How does this boredom-free 'living absolutely in the present' come about? At first glance you'd think life as an Australian Aboriginal, living in the pre-settlement Outback, would be pretty tedious, what with the unrelenting heat, the diet of lizards and witchety grubs, and the unchanging blandness of the Bore Track landscape. But consider this. The act of concentrating on survival, with all of the complex lore that this entailed, would have minimized the opportunities for boredom to strike. Perhaps such a life would have involved round-the-clock concentration and round-the-clock movement. Survival in a waterless and dangerous environment like pre-settlement

Australia meant learning by heart a vast amount of survival lore: animal habits, animal tracks and their routes, waterholes, 'maps' of safe human and animal migration routes, as well as having an understanding of the seasonal variation of edible flora, of all of the non-animal food sources, and of how safely to prepare and ingest them. The list of crucial life-saving items could go on and on. Is there room in such a precarious world for the lack of vigilance that boredom would entail?

This drawing, from the turn of the nineteenth century, depicts the tooth-rapping ceremony. It was performed near

22 Tooth-rapping ceremony

Farm Cove in Sydney and it was part of an all-night initiation ritual. The boy at the centre of the picture is being held while a man knocks out one of his front teeth. Geographical and vegetal lore that was crucial to the survival of the Australian Aboriginals appears to have been attached to 'religious' rituals such as this. Traditional teachings were embedded in mytho-logical tales, and their details imparted in the course of initia-tion rites such as this one. Horrendous practices such as tooth rapping, scarring with hot coals, circumcision, infibulation, beatings, flesh and skin piercing, and the strict observance of ritual thereafter, ensured that all of this life-saving mythical information was remembered exactly.

The medical anthropologist H.D. Eastwell provides a straightforward and helpful explanation of these rituals. He discusses subincision – the opening with a sharpened stone knife of the urethral passage of a man's penis from below – which the initiant underwent fully awake. The practice had no medical or health-related benefit. Rather, as Eastwell explains, the operation 'takes place in the context of the teaching of the myths to initiate and that these myths provide, in coded form, information on the geographic location of vital waterholes. The painful operation is then regarded as reinforcing the learning of this essential information.' Successful daily life – surviving, that is – may have meant repeating religiously these rituals just as each geographical context demanded. In this sense life really is 'living absolutely in the present': that present is the eternal or cyclical repetition of ritual. It's perhaps too speculative to guess the extent to which ritual shaped all of the experience of the indigenous. But it appears likely that the mantras of ritual are re-enacted each day and each hour, even each minute, and this enables their unremitting internalization. Ritual can fill out a life.

Rituals may minimize the opportunities for the sort of empty time on which boredom feeds to develop, both physically (in having to perform them) and mentally. Rituals can create for the simplest of actions (rising in the morning, how you eat a meal) a busy-ness that precludes empty, private time. These people weren't just 'living absolutely in the present', but living in the ghostly world of ritual where time does not exist except in the circular sense and where all action is a repetition of mythological precedent. It is hard to imagine how in such a 'busy' world there would be any place left for boredom.

This of course is supposition. We cannot get inside the minds of the preliterate. While it is very compelling, the notion that 'living absolutely in the present' exempts a person from boredom is not completely convincing. Let's put the problem another way. Can you be bored if you have no sense of past time? Perhaps if you are 'living absolutely in the present' then personal memory, by which people these days set so much store, is not so vital. These days people tend to dip in and out of the memory bank as they choose or as health allows. It's fair to say that modern societies use memory in a recreational manner. Most people draw great pleasure from thinking back over the more enjoyable elements of their lives. But I guess that, if you are 'living absolutely in the present', you do not.

The ghostly ritual world of the preliterate has no easy parallel in modern experience. Let's not try to seek a parallel. But it is easy enough to imagine what the experience now for those with no sense of past time might be. Perhaps it is closer to that of Cyril, Angus Lordie's pet dog in Alexander McCall Smith's *Love over Scotland* (2006): 'and there was that familiar smell, the one he had smelled in Valvona & Crolla that day – when was it? He had no idea whether it was a long time ago, for dogs have no sense of past time, but he had smelled it in that place.' Cyril's memory might be acute in an olfactory and spatial sense, but it's chronologically weak. Can you be bored if, like Cyril, you are 'living absolutely in the present?' Of course. Cyril would have periodically suffered confinement, repetitious experiences, and satiety; in other words the usual preconditions for a creature to have a sense of being bored. They don't rely on a strong sense of time or sequence – though, as has been seen, boredom itself has strange effects on the perception of time.

I am not sure whether or not it is true to say that preliterate societies 'live in the moment', but I am fairly certain that 'living in the moment' does not make anyone immune from boredom. Boredom has a natural biological basis, just like depression. It can be seen in other humans who are constrained to the moment, such as those suffering from dementia.

As I have stated previously, what may vary is the degree to which boredom can play a role in human life. It seems probable that some societies may have no space for boredom. But to me it also seems probable that some societies or even some individuals may express boredom through other emotions or emotional registers. Different cultures may express (write about, show, and even feel) boredom in markedly different manners. Other affective states may certainly be expressed differently. Depression, for example, was for a time expressed in

China as a type of nerve disease or neurasthenia. The medical anthropologist, Arthur Kleinman believed this coincided with the Chinese Cultural Revolution when depression was considered 'bourgeois', and thus the affective state became more acceptable if it was transferred from the mind to the body. In Latin, depression can be termed a four-day fever (the so called quartan fever), similarly lending this mental disturbance a corporeal quality. And boredom itself can assume some pretty strange descriptors. In Latin it can be termed *veternus* or 'old age'. Whether this is because the aged are seen as being boring, or because boredom can make a person sluggish and slow, I do not know. In ancient Greek the term for boredom, *alus*, means something like 'otherness'. Perhaps this hints at the way bored individuals can seem distracted and other to their normal mental state.

* * *

Nostalgia seems to be another of these synonyms – or evasive descriptors – for the feeling that you're bored. Nostalgia might be thought to manifest itself in a bored person's emotional repertoire when, more through reflex than intent, their mind drifts back to happier, more exciting times in their life. Remembered places and occasions, real or imagined, historical or fantastic, can offer an antidote to the tedium of the present. I'm sure that most people would prefer to admit to this sentimental and slightly romantic yearning for a less boring past than to say that they are simply bored. But the close link between the two is undeniable.

Unfortunately, the very act of remembering better times may make the present seem even drearier. Disgust, once again, has an important role to play here. The concocted Greek word, nostalgia, literally means homesickness. That makes sense. The objects of nostalgia are often related to home or to childhood, or to a time when the sufferer felt happier, more rooted, 'at home' – but that biliousness reminds us that the yearning for past time is based on a feeling of mild disgust with the present. Boredom is founded on this too.

It's no secret that literature and visual art are crowded with representations of this wistful habit of mentally revisiting happier and earlier or even primordial times: the myths of the Golden Age or the Age of Saturn or of the Eternal Return, in the grand versions, or any books that evoke the possibilities of homecoming and the establishment of harmony. In classical antiquity there is a very large literature devoted to myths of return and Golden Ages – to the expression, that is, of the feeling of nostalgia, even though they lacked the term for it. This fascination with the Golden Age might well be the product of crisis periods. As Fred Davis, the sociologist of nostalgia, has suggested: 'mass nostalgia reactions are most likely to occur in the wake of periods of severe cultural discontinuity, as happened following the profound identity upheavals of the nineteen-sixties'. But then again, it may be another way by which boredom can be felt, expressed, or at least imagined. Indeed, boredom often motivates this desire to escape into the cheerful realms of fantasy.

René Magritte's *Homesickness* (1940) is a very well known picture, although its fame has done noting to modulate its quiet mystery. It is a profoundly allusive work, and one which plays on the theme of nostalgia and unexpected analogies for boredom.

23 René Magritte, *Le Mal du Pays* (*Homesickness*), 1940

The angel seems utterly bored. Perhaps the earthly high life is not all it's cracked up to be. Dressed in what looks like a dinner suit, the angel could be on the way home after an expensive evening out. Is he locked into the dull social round that requires of the celestial the mundane accoutrements of the wealthy middle class? The bridge offers a hint of a symbolic link between worlds, although the descending mist and drab sky make the whole scene claustrophobic. Is he about to jump? Magritte's title suggests instead that the angel is homesick, and rather keen to get back to his normal heavenly routines.

The lion may hold the key to the puzzle of this painting. This hairy beast doesn't belong on the bridge; still less should it be resting its left paw in such an odd position. It is designed to recall to the viewer the legend of St Jerome, who tamed a ravaging lion by removing a painful thorn from its pad. This story from the Golden Legend has inspired numerous artists down the centuries: Albrecht Dürer, for one, and sixty years before *Melencolia I,* Jan van Eyck, who painted not only the recumbent, upturned-pawed lion, but also a resolutely bored St Jerome seated at his desk. Like Dürer's angel of melancholia, Van Eyck's Jerome is suffering the boredom brought on by too much intellectual study. Is Magritte's black-suited angel also cupping his head in his hand, just out of sight? In this strange and apparently hallucinatory painting combining a posed angel and the (dare I say bored-looking) lion, Magritte seems deliberately to be tapping into a visual tradition which connects melancholia, homesickness and boredom.

Indications of boredom suffuse Magritte's painting. The sky is an awful bright fawn colour – a nauseous colour if ever there was one. The angel's gaze away from us could well be of the Antarctic variety. His posture echoes that of Böcklin's Odysseus, another victim of boredom. And if the gaze of that patristic lion does not resemble that of Hegeso, I'll be surprised. The theme of *Homesickness* and the emotion it attempts to convey is homesickness – but the imagery is all of boredom.

24 Jan van Eyck, *St Jerome in his Study, c.* 1435

Lucas Cranach the Elder's *The Golden Age* seems the very obverse of Magritte's doleful evocation of the relationship between nostalgia and boredom. It depicts all the fun of the Golden Age. Everyone is naked, Adams and Eves, dancing round an apple tree in the verdant walled garden, or skinny dipping, or languorously discussing philosophy. There are no heads slumping on hands, and no long stares into nothingness: all the

25 Lucas Cranach the Elder, *The Golden Age, c.* 1530

people in this painting – and there are lots of them – look at one another. Cranach's lions are playing, not gloomy like Magritte's staring creature. With no horizon visible, infinity too has been banished. Their seeming entrapment within the high walls of this luxurious garden may represent the only hint of boredom.

The exuberant world evoked in this painting, is built, like most things nostalgic, on fantasy. The fantasy is that there could have been a Golden Age at some time in the past, or that there might be one in the future. Is the fantasy a product of an era and a consciousness in crisis, something of the order of Norman Cohn's millenarianism in his famous and influential *The Pursuit of the Millennium* (1957)? Or does *The Golden Age* draw its power from offering solace for the bored and the estranged? It is not possible to adjudicate on the opinions of Lucas Cranach the Elder, but what of our own attitudes? Don't we still wish for the whole gamut of peace and harmony (as well as sex) that this painting depicts? It is drearily unlike this in the economically depressed real world. How boring most lives seem in contrast. When did you last go skinny dipping? This vivaciously utopian painting represents an extreme form of nostalgia and, rather than offering solace, it makes the viewer all the more aware of the boredom that is so often just round the corner. It's boredom rather than crisis that allows this painting to resonate so much with modern viewers.

For Cranach's contemporaries, myths of the Eternal Return and of the Golden Age abounded, as they did in other pre-industrial and sometimes preliterate cultures. It's been my experience that these are the very cultures that lack specific terms for boredom. It was not that they were not necessarily bored, but maybe that they felt 'I'm bored' in a different way.

* * *

Does boredom have a history? It all depends on what you mean by boredom. If it's the simple boredom to which humans and animals, the articulate and the inarticulate, the young and the old seem to be prone, then the answer is a yes and a no. It's an emotion, and emotions are constants throughout history. But, as I have suggested, in some circumstances it's possible that simple boredom plays less of a role: in preliterate and in some pre-industrial societies its importance may be occluded by an overpowering presence of ritual. And in others, perhaps those that prefer to explain the intangible aspects of emotion through the body, it may be expressed in different ways – as nostalgia, or homesickness, or utopianism.

But if it's existential boredom that is at issue, the answer is less clear. Most discussions of this 'boredom' deem this depression-like state to date from the time of the European Enlightenment. The great changes that took place at this time are often said to be responsible for a number of other conditions partly related to boredom: leisure, our sense of self, our sense of time, madness, depression, friendship, and even such literary motifs as the double. So, why not? If such a thing as 'existential boredom' exists, that is. Sceptics like me might prefer to see it as a name for a constellation of other disorders, or simply a relatively trivial phenomenon. Even Jean-Paul Sartre – lauded by many as the grandfather of existential boredom after *Nausea*, perhaps the most evocative literary portrait of it ever, was published in 1938 – turned his back on the condition. In an interview in 1964 he observed: 'I have seen children die of hunger. In front of a dying child, *Nausea* has no weight.'

Boredom is a universal experience, and it's been felt in most eras. For the most part, as we've seen, it's a beneficial emotion. But it is not always pleasant, especially if it becomes chronic. Are there means by which its worst aspects can be mitigated? Some of the answers to this query are offered, once again, by the neurologists. And some of the best answers can be found in old age homes. Let's see how.

6

The long march back to boredom

MERVYN KING KNOWS where boredom's proper place is. This was in October 2008 in the midst of the credit crunch. As the governor of the Bank of England, he entreated financiers to be more patient: 'I have said many times that successful monetary policy would appear rather boring,' he stated. 'So let me extend an invitation to the banking industry to join me in promoting the idea that a little more boredom would be no bad thing. The long march back to boredom and stability starts tonight in Leeds.'

Boredom is a normal, useful, and an incredibly common part of human experience. Like Mervyn King I often think that everyone should have more of it and, like the governor, I also think that everyone should be less impatient with it. My own long march back to boredom will start with the brain.

What is boredom's place? I mean this quite literally. Whereabouts in the brain is boredom experienced? There are good grounds for guessing that it occurs inside the region called the insular cortex. The insula, as it is normally known, is

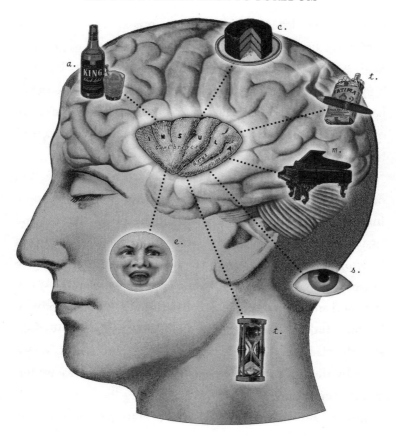

26 Insula illustration

the size of a large kalamata olive. It's situated towards the
bottom of the cranium, near the brainstem. Neuroscientists
believe that it is one of the keys to the understanding of how
it is that humans are able to feel that they are human. In
functional imaging experiments researchers have discovered
that the insula lights up, according to Sandra Blakeslee, 'when
people crave drugs, feel pain, empathize with others, listen
to jokes, see disgust on someone's face, are shunned in

171

social settings, listen to music, decide not to buy an item, see someone cheat and decide to punish them, and determine degrees of preference while eating chocolate'. To be even more precise, neuroscientists have discovered that the insula has an important role in pain perception and in the experience of a number of basic emotions. These include anger, fear, happiness, sadness and disgust.

All mammals seem to have an insular cortex. The function of the insula is to read and to monitor body condition. Information relating to the status of the body's organs and tissues is carried from the receptors along spinal pathways. It ends up via the brainstem in the insula, where there are two sensory areas. The anterior insula appears to relate to smell, taste and emotion, whereas the posterior insula relates more to hearing and to bodily function. In the insula, the various stimuli at large in the world that have been perceived as sensations by the body are here transformed into what are understood as emotions.

Just imagine the stench of a barrel of rotting anchovies. The sensations relating to that piscine pong are transmitted to the nose, then from the nose via the spinal pathways and right up to the anterior insula. The insula processes the stinking external information and produces an emotion that will match human sensory experience – in this case, vigorous disgust. The same process applies for the other primary emotions such as happiness, sadness, fear, anger and surprise, and at least forms the basis for secondary emotions such as sympathy, embarrassment, shame, guilt, pride, jealousy, envy, gratitude, admiration, indignation and contempt. Boredom, as has been seen, is an emotion connected to the primary emotion of disgust, and it has a special relationship to the insular cortex.

Dr Arthur D. Craig of the Burrow Neurological Institute in Phoenix speculates that the insula 'may also be involved in the human sense of the progress of time'. Dr Craig hypothesizes that the insula may be capable of producing 'an anticipatory signal of how people may feel as opposed to how they feel now'. He wonders if this is why highly charged emotional experiences, love and infatuation for example, can affect the human sense of time. Time can stand still in such moments. Craig believes that sensation takes place in the insula, a region of the brain that stands at 'a crossroads of time and desire'.

It is very suggestive. Certainly time acts as an emotional register as much for boredom as it does for desire – it drags, it speeds up, it can heal and it can harm. And if the emotion of boredom can be linked to the function of the insula, then perhaps this may help to explain the peculiar relationship that exists between boredom and time. The early Christian writer and ascetic Evagrius observed how boredom can actually alter the perceptions of time: 'this demon makes the sun appear sluggish and immobile, just as if the length of the day were fifty hours'. In fact the experience of the world at that time seems to move so slowly that it's often as if you stand right outside of it. Is it the insula that endows boredom with this warped temporality? Could the insula stand at the crossroads of time and boredom?

Boredom's connection to disgust, and its intriguing links to the alterations of its sufferers' sense of temporality, hint that boredom may well be produced within the insula. The problem is that researchers are looking elsewhere. For example, in Daniel Weissman's boredom experiment at the University of Michigan (mentioned in the Preface) where volunteers in an MRI room were asked to identify letters as they appeared on a screen, the scientists focused on the areas of the brain closely related to self-control, vision and language processing and on those intervals when the concentration of the volunteers slipped. What if they looked instead at the insula? This might finally settle the emotional status of boredom. If the insula did light up, it might provide some evidentiary basis for a connection between the insula and boredom.

Boredom exists, I have argued, to provide an early warning signal that certain situations may be dangerous to our well-being. Like disgust, it seems to be an adaptive emotion. It exists to help you prosper. Just as disgust stops you from dipping into that barrel of rotting anchovies to add to your *salade niçoise*, so boredom, in social settings, alerts you to situations that can do no psychological good. It is there to encourage people to adapt their behaviour to protect them from social toxins, just as its first cousin disgust is designed, biologically speaking, to cause people to adapt their behaviour to real physical toxins. Maybe boredom should be viewed in the way that gout or angina sometimes is – as a sign of worse things to follow unless there's a change in lifestyle.

Boredom needs no cure, that's the logic of what I am saying. Like all the adaptive emotions that have come up, it seems that boredom has its uses. The best 'cure' for boredom, therefore, is to follow the advice of the emotion and to walk away from the situation that is provoking it. It would be best that we think not in terms of a cure for boredom but rather in terms of heeding the advice that the emotion is trying to signal. But it is not always possible to walk away from boredom. If you are stuck in economy on a plane between London and Sydney, there is no getting out.

When it's impossible to walk away from boredom, what can you do? Are there any practical remedies that may be brought into play against boredom to prevent it from mutating into something more harmful and sinister? If your disposition is one that is prone to or even driven to boredom – if, say, you are an extroverted male, or if you have a very dull job, or if you have an unavoidably dreary home life, or if you are unemployed – then a cure becomes a very pressing need.

Where do you find help? Not from a doctor. A doctor would laugh if you said that you needed a little something for your boredom. Neither is boredom part of a psychiatrist's brief. Psychologists might give you this advice: 'individuals in an undesired state of boredom may benefit by recognizing their predilection towards negative affect and correcting their inaccurate cognition before they develop into an obdurate and deleterious style of thinking that may lead to a distancing of themselves from not only friends and family, but reality as well'.

The simplest of all methods is doubtless what a grandmother would prescribe: variety in experience. Such a variety should protect not just against boredom, but also against the agitation, anger and the depression that can follow on from unchecked chronic boredom. I have spoken to many people who will admit to being chronically bored. As you'd expect, they are mostly working in my profession and their cures are rather on the cerebral side. What do they do to try to bail out? They try to keep as many interests as possible on the go: books, politics, exercise, dromomania, art galleries, teaching, music, collecting, family when they have it, cooking, as much comedy as possible.

There seems to be a solid biological basis for this claim that variety can cure boredom. Norman Doidge, in his book on neural plasticity entitled *The Brain that Changes Itself*, points out that experimental research on rats has shown that stimulation produces a positive effect on their brains. Stimulated rats' brains had more neurotransmitters, were heavier and had a better blood supply than the brains of rats in less stimulating environments. Norman Doidge maintains that the same is true for the human brain. 'Enriched environments,' he points out, 'strengthen the brain.' Stimulation and enrichment are the direct antitheses of boredom. Doidge goes on to say that 'nothing speeds brain atrophy more than being immobilized in the same environment: the monotony undermines our dopamine and attentional systems crucial to maintaining brain plasticity. A cognitively rich physical activity . . . [will] have the added benefit of being social, which also preserves brain health.' Variety and stimulation, he explains, encourage neurogenesis, the actual regrowth of brain cells. And further, variety and stimulation can actually extend the life of the neurons in the hippocampus. It is one of those beneficially vicious circles. Monotony literally shrinks the brain by reducing the number and life span of its neurons. Enrichment, by increasing neuronal numbers and life spans, may decrease one's proneness to boredom. It appears to be the case that, whatever your genetic proneness to boredom, enrichment and stimulation – variety – seem both to strengthen the brain and to see off boredom.

It's also possible that music is a more powerful source of enrichment and stimulation than might have been expected. It may even cure boredom. Evidence comes from one of the most unexpected of quarters: the mighty elephants of Belfast Zoo. Researchers from Queen's University Belfast, led by Dr Deborah Wells, have observed that playing classical music reduces abnormal behaviour in elephants. Swaying, pacing and trunk tossing are all minimized when the tuskers listen to Mozart.

Just how Dr Wells went about the experiment is fascinating to learn. Her team watched the behaviour of four female Asian elephants for four hours each day and over three five-day periods. Recording the elephants' reactions every minute during these test periods, it's a wonder that Dr Wells did not fall prone to an attack of chronic boredom herself. During the first five-day period the animals were given no music to listen to, in the second period they were played CDs of Mozart, Handel, Elgar and Beethoven, and in the third period the music was turned off again. The team observed a decrease in the frequency of abnormal behaviour while they were playing music, and it did not interfere with normal healthy activities such as feeding. Dr Wells and her team have also carried out this sort of experiment with dogs and gorillas. 'Classical [music] had the most beneficial effect,' Dr Wells explained. 'Heavy metal had quite an adverse effect on the dogs.'

The 'stereotypic patterns of behaviour' displayed by the elephants, as Dr Wells pointed out in a *Guardian* article on the experiment, are caused by the captive elephants' 'inherent instinct to roam vast distances'. The unsettled behaviour of these insula-endowed pachyderms was a reaction to their temporarily unavoidable, certainly unchosen, and totally predictable conditions: to their boring situation, in other words. The swaying and pacing were the first step in the elephants' reaction against boredom, which could then escalate to more deleterious reactions such as agitation, anger and depression. So, if music works to allay the reactions to boredom, it's not unreasonable to speculate that it would alleviate boredom itself. These experiments have not yet been replicated in humans and I would make no conjectures as to the type of music that would work. Dogs may not like heavy metal, but Charles Snowdon from the University of Wisconsin at Madison and his colleague David Teie of the University of Maryland have reported that chimps enjoy Metallica.

Another putative cure for boredom is the unlikely but wholesome candidate of aerobic exercise. The information comes from Sue Halpern's recent book, *Can't Remember What I Forgot* (2008), which has as its focus the loss of memory in old age, especially when this is derived from dementia. The 'good news' of Halpern's subtitle is not editorial hype, but real science. During the years Halpern was writing this book, one definite means of neurogenesis – brain cell regrowth – came to light. This was aerobic exercise. The mechanics of the process are quite straightforward: exercise promotes new cell growth in old brains by increasing their blood volume, and cell growth improves memory. It was true for mice with cognitive impairment and it was true for humans with mild cognitive impairment. It didn't remove the amyloid plaque that causes Alzheimer's Disease, but it improved cognition anyway. Sue Halpern explains some of the details:

> Exercise . . . increased the amount of the chemical BDNF (brain derived neurotrophic factor) circulating in the brain, and it was BDNF that stimulated the birth of new brain cells . . . BDNF also enhanced neural plasticity, which was to say that it enabled the brain to prosper. In diseases like Alzheimer's, depression, Parkinson's, and dementia more generally, BDNF levels were low. In people who exercised BDNF levels rose.

Again and again in this book the link between boredom and depression has been made. If the chemical BDNF ameliorates depression by stimulating the birth of new brain cells and by enhancing neural plasticity, so too may BDNF ameliorate boredom, especially the chronic form.

Social interaction may also play a part. In this case the evidence comes from the parallels between depression, the plight of the ageing brain and that of the chronically bored. A recent article in the *New York Times* on memory retention in the very old (24 May 2009) emphasized the social dimension of neural plasticity. Of a group of nonagenarians living in a retirement village in Laguna Woods, California, whose memory seems quite remarkably unimpaired, the author of the piece, Benedict Carey, tells us:

> 'These are the most successful agers on earth, and they're only just beginning to teach us what's important, in their

genes, in their routines, in their lives,' said Dr. Claudia
Kawas, a neurologist at the University of California, Irvine.
'We think, for example, that it's very important to use your
brain, to keep challenging your mind, but all mental activities may not be equal. We're seeing some evidence that a
social component may be crucial.'

My late Auntie Madge, who kept her memory intact to a fair
old age, used to claim that there were two secrets: 'keep on
doing the crossword and keep talking to people'. Crosswords
meant intellectual activity and talking to people meant the
social component stressed by Dr Kawas. Sociability seems to
assist the brain in retaining its neural plasticity. I realize that it
seems thumpingly obvious to say that social interaction may
assist in the amelioration of chronic boredom, but its encouragement of neural plasticity provides a possible scientific basis
for Auntie Madge's old saw.

Music and aerobic exercise and community: it sounds
rather like the cornerstone elements for the education of
the elite if Plato's *Republic* were a modern suburban gym.
However corny these three cures may look, they do offer very
practical means by which chronic boredom may be relieved.
And I would stress practical. These three palliatives – music
and aerobic exercise and social interaction – taken separately,
offer means that could be used right now to counteract chronic
boredom.

One last suggestion is derived from the work of Françoise
Wemelsfelder whose studies on boredom in animals have done
so much to unravel the perplexities of the matter. Wemelsfelder

suggests in her article 'Animal Boredom' that 'functional behavior' (performing the activities, such as foraging, that come naturally in the wild) and the avoidance of boredom (what she calls 'voluntary attention') 'are two sides of the same coin and that . . . it is not useful to distinguish functionally motivated behavior from what "animals like to do"'. So it is that something as simple as feeding is for an animal 'a meaningful goal'. Enriched environments are additional aids, but the encouragement of normal functional behaviour in itself seems to discourage boredom. It's easy to see how this might work for humans. Resolute attention to the necessary rituals of daily life (eating regularly, work, sleep, family) may well mitigate chronic boredom. Wemelsfelder suggests that the best way to obviate boredom may be 'to enhance the animal's [or human's] active, creative role in organizing its own life'.

And so it is that curing boredom seems to be related to managing empty time. Apart from Wemelsfelder's counter-intuitive insight, the most obvious counter-measure to enforced boredom is the capacity to use empty time well, to be able to turn empty time into enjoyable free time. Let's call this enjoyable free time leisure time. Of all of the cures for boredom that I have been mentioning in this chapter, this one definitely entails long-term engagement.

What is it, then, to be able to use empty time and leisure time well? It's still very hard to better the reliable Aristotle's description of leisure and of how empty time might best be used. For Aristotle leisure time constituted an activity that was pleasurable (there must be a play element in things – Françoise Wemelsfelder links the disappearance of 'inquisitive play' to chronic boredom), represented an end in itself (it's the opposite of work), involved engagement with other people (there's my Auntie Madge 'talking to people'), and should also entail the use of both the body and, in particular, the mind (there's the component of neural plasticity). How do some of our most treasured leisure activities fare against this description?

Travel – no, it's usually designed as an escape from work. It isn't an end in itself, unless you can put a bizarre twist on it. The *Independent* (29 January 1994) reported that Michael Mellor, then 27, of Greenwich became so bored at weekends that he dressed up as a traffic policeman and travelled the M25 'stopping motorists and ticking them off'. I have not been able to find out the result of his hearing at Guildford, Surrey in the same year, but I am sure Mr Mellor's remedy was an effective one.

And what of watching television? Does this constitute leisure? Never: no brain and no body. Sport? Sometimes, but if it's too competitive, then it has an end in mind, the defeat of others. Sex – maybe, if there's no procreation intended, but it's a stretch to imagine that the mind is involved, despite the neural plasticity encouraged by this popular aerobic activity. Conversation? It's usually mindless. Cards or board games? These are good candidates. Robert Burton in *The Anatomy of Melancholy* recommended cards and board games in the battle against ennui, and Boswell urged a similar remedy on Dr Johnson. But the same caveats apply to cards and board games as to sport. The activities must have not an end in themselves. Any activities, even competitive sports, that are end driven represent, in Aristotle's scheme of things, different versions of work. For work, after all, would not be work if it did not have a practical end in mind. And work is the opposite of leisure.

Since the Protestant Reformation we have golloped down the notion that activities that are to be valued should be immediately practical. They should even be moral. This spirit of moral practicality has infected leisure by insisting on the practical and the moral as its basis. Thus such-and-such a leisure activity becomes valued because it is good for the body, or good for the mind, or good for the family, or good for the community. Or, woe betide, good for God. So novels and poetry are bad, biography and self-help are good. Cards are bad, football is good. And so it goes. The popular German-American cultural critic Theodor Adorno, who made his mark on the theory of leisure, takes the conversation beyond Protestantism. 'Free Time', admittedly one of his odder essays, alarmingly links TV with sunbathing, camping holidays and boredom. Most free time is shaped by the demands of work, Adorno believes. But he sees the controlling agent as commerce. Time off, for Adorno, is driven by the same commercialization as is time-on: work generates profits, and so must free time. Theodor Adorno believes that this is why North Americans like me spend a fortune on free time. And maybe, he suggests, that is why we become so bored so often when we are on holiday. North Americans turned free time back into work time. Remember the postcard I received from a friend last August? It read: 'Had a wonderful holiday. Rained the whole time. Didn't have to take the children to the beach once. Got buckets of work done.'

27 Theodor Adorno

Leisure time should be impractical, amoral, pleasurable and sociable. What does all this have to do with boredom? It looks very much as if the current notion of leisure, because it's so tied in with work, is doomed to generate boredom. How could it not? If work is boring, then leisure, as a variant of work, must be boring too. If leisure time is to become a boredom-free zone, then it'll have to concern itself with activities that have no practical, moral or commercial ends. Perhaps Tim Winton has caught the idea best in his marvellous novel *Breath* (2008) when he describes surfing, the book's preeminent leisure activity, as 'something completely pointless and beautiful'.

Boredom is a very good thing to be able to escape, but it should never be trivialized. No emotion can be treated as a trivial thing. That's because it's through the emotions that we humans come to know the world and come to know ourselves. I've mentioned the adaptive capacity of boredom sufficiently so to this extent the usefulness of the emotion should be clear. But boredom has other positive characteristics as well.

Because it can breed dissatisfaction with views and concepts that are intellectually shop worn, boredom can encourage creativity. Boredom may drive thinkers and artists to question the accepted and to search for change. This can even be the case for schoolchildren, according to Teresa Belton and Esther Priyadharshini in their fascinating survey article 'Boredom and Schooling'. They believe that boredom 'can also contain critical reflective potential and can be a powerful stimulus to creativity [for students]'. They suggest that 'a certain amount of boredom [in classrooms], by allowing for contemplation, daydreaming and imagining alternatives, allows a refreshed return to activity'. And they go on to cite approvingly a US study 'of the subjective experience of boredom of 170 US college students aged 19- to 56-years-old [which] revealed that 73% of the participants believed that boredom could sometimes be positive, especially as an opportunity for thought and reflection or relaxation'.

Although boredom is never an easy emotion to tolerate, it has always had this curious connection with creativity. The clichés abound on this topic. Samuel Johnson is said to have stayed in bed dulled and bored daily till midday or later. He showed no public shame concerning this habit, but, as his letters show, he remonstrated with himself privately over what he saw as a failing. Who ever feels easy with their boredom? Samuel Johnson was *still* able to compose 1,800 words of prose per hour. The brilliant scientific deductions of Sir Arthur Conan Doyle's Sherlock Holmes were interspersed with periods of boredom and lethargy. The detective escapes the tedium – as have many other dopamine-deficient individuals – by taking drugs. Conan Doyle did not believe that either the boredom or the remedy blunted his superior intellect one iota. The great poet Joseph Brodsky makes grand claims for the value of his own persistent boredom: 'When hit by boredom, let yourself be crushed by it; submerge, hit bottom. In general, with things unpleasant, the rule is: The sooner you hit bottom, the faster you surface. The idea here is to exact a full look at the worst. The reason boredom deserves such scrutiny is that it represents pure, undiluted time in all its repetitive, redundant, monotonous splendor.'

Of course claims such as these need nuance. If the boredom is intractable and if it is without end, then there's certain to be trouble. Boredom may be tolerable, but chronic boredom is too enervating for even the most creative and it can spill over into agitation, anger and depression. But Brodsky touches on another positive side to boredom that's sometimes mentioned: it can allow you to be yourself. Boredom, it is said, drives a wedge between you and the world around, and so it tends to drive a sufferer back in on themselves. For Antoine Roquentin in Sartre's *Nausea*, boredom allowed him to find a clearer sense of his place within the world. Roquentin came to the conclusion that there is no necessary connection between an individual and the world about: living is just 'to be there'.

Boredom can sometimes make a person stand apart from other people, from the world and, odd as it is to say, even stand apart from themselves. Boredom intensifies self-perception. In fact boredom offers an unusual and rare enforced opportunity to see yourself as another – it doesn't happen when you're having a noisy party after football with the team in F.A.T.S. Bar & Grill. Such contemplation, thanks to boredom, is not necessarily a mind-altering experience. Getting a sense of yourself, paradoxically, can be quite a boring pursuit.

I suspect that no one should be too enthusiastic about the therapeutic benefits of boredom. They are easily exaggerated. Dunbar, in Joseph Heller's *Catch-22* (1961) for example, cultivates boredom because it appears to slow time, and could make his living days seem twice as long as they ought to be. Flying missions over Italy nearing the end of the Second World War, Dunbar's life is perpetually threatened. For him, boredom offers a therapy for fear of death. But I don't find that too convincing. Albert Speer tried the reverse tactic to try to speed along his prison sentence, but it can hardly have helped: '*March 24, 1947*: Now I have reached twelve hours of sleep daily. If I can keep that up I shall be cutting my imprisonment by a full five years – by comparison with my normal sleeping time of six hours.' Not for a minute do I believe that this was effective.

* * *

Boredom is a much easier and a more *boring* emotion than it is ever given credit for. Much of my attention has been given to the more neglected simple form – it is definitely the more dreary of the two. It's claimed that children and old people have it. Clever people suffer from the complex or existential version. Or so they think: intellectuals are rather keen to have a special, cerebral name for their complaint: existential boredom has a nice ring to it.

Depression is the reason why these versions of boredom have become so muddled. This is because depression links the two kinds – as one extremity in the cycle of depression, boredom and mania that unalleviated simple boredom can give rise to; and as a component element in the grab-bag condition that is existential boredom, an element that perhaps describes it better than 'boredom'. We have seen that the imagery and language of boredom can be easily confused with various depressive states: the head in the hand gesture is perhaps the most obvious example. And here is one more: what's the matter with the person described here – depression or existential boredom?

He feels solitary, indescribably unhappy, as a 'creature disinherited of fate'; he is sceptical about God, and with a certain dull submission, which shuts out every comfort and every gleam of light, he drags himself with difficulty from one day to another. Everything has become disagreeable to him; everything wearies him, company, music, travel, his professional work. Everywhere he sees only the dark side and difficulties; the people around him are not so good and unselfish as he thought; one disappointment and disillusionment follows another. Life appears to him to be aimless, he thinks that he is superfluous to the world, he cannot constrain himself any longer, the thought occurs to him to take his life without knowing why. He has a feeling as if something has cracked in him.

This is not someone in the throes of an attack of existential boredom. It is one of the founders of modern psychiatry Emil Kraepelin's description of a depressive, dating from 1921. It's so easy to muddle up existential boredom with depression. And it's easy to muddle up simple boredom with existential boredom. There really does need to be another word for that latter, limelight-stealing, mongrel condition.

This all leads right back to my friend David Londey and his clever observation that maybe there is no such thing as boredom at all. Well, there is and there isn't. What I've suggested in this book is that David Londey's intuition best applies to existential boredom. That form has got something more to do with depression and melancholia than with the emotion that a small child feels when kept inside on a sunny day – when, instead of playing messily outside in the sandpit, they are confronted by a temporarily unavoidable and repetitious set of circumstances. Indoors. Existential boredom is neither an emotion, nor a mood, nor a feeling. Rather, it is better thought of as an impressive intellectual formulation. It's something to which intellectuals believe they are especially prone. The less kind would have said, bluntly, that they were depressed. But simple boredom does exist – and in fact is experienced far more frequently than people are willing to admit, for to admit to suffering boredom is to admit to being childish. But boredom has a lot going for it. It is useful and it has existed since time immemorial. Admittedly some societies seem relatively immune to boredom, but at what cost? I would not like to inhabit the unthinking world of the ritual past. Self-consciousness, self-questioning have no place in such rigid worlds. Better the boredom that has dogged all societies that are not dependent for their survival on mythical lore.

There has been quite a lot written lately concerning the over-medicalizing of emotional states such as shyness and sadness. Shyness, Christopher Lane explains in his book of the same name, is reread as a social anxiety disorder, then is treated with a variety of antidepressants. Sadness, argue Allan Horowitz and Jerome Wakefield in *The Loss of Sadness*, becomes clinical depression and is dealt with in the same manner. Neither emotion requires such treatment – they are a normal part of human experience. Boredom too has perhaps suffered in the same way by being transformed into a philosophical sickness. There is no need to dismiss the emotion as childish, as the sign of laziness or an idle mind, or, worse still in my opinion, to render it alarmingly significant by endowing it with philosophical accoutrements. Boredom is a normal, useful, and incredibly common part of human experience. That many of us suffer it should be no cause for embarrassment. Boredom simply deserves respect for the, well, boring experience that it is.

Readings

Preface

Boredom is often in the news: Nic Marks' verdict on the place of boredom in British life was discussed in BBC/NEWS 24 January 2009 and Daniel Weissman's scientific work was reported in the *New Scientist*, 13 December 2008. These two pieces set the scene for the more substantial work of, for example, Lars Svendsen, a prolific, engaging and gifted author. His *A Philosophy of Boredom* (London: Reaktion Books, 2005) is the most interesting book on the subject but, as the title suggests, primarily focuses on boredom as a philosophical emotion. (Elements of his categorization – situational boredom and existential boredom – derive from Martin Doehlemann's *Langeweile?: Deutung eines verbreiteten Phänomens* [Boredom: The Interpretation of a Widespread Phenomenon], Frankfurt, 1991). Svendsen touches on the subject of boredom again in some of his other books, notably in *Work* (Stocksfield: Acumen, 2008), and, unexpectedly, in *Fashion: A Philosophy* (London: Reaktion Books, 2006), where he pays more attention to the childish, simple form of boredom. Boredom seems to have a special link to Scandinavia: a fascinating and completely unexpected application of Svendsen's and Doehlemann's thinking is Bård

Mæland and Paul Otto Brunstad's *Enduring Military Boredom: From 1750 to the Present* (London: Palgrave Macmillan, 2009).

A good place to look at the connection between boredom and depression is in Andrew Solomon's *The Noonday Demon: An Atlas of Depression* (New York: Scribner, 2001). The connections of boredom to religion are sensitively explored in Michael Raposa's *Boredom and the Religious Imagination* (Charlottesville: University Press of Virginia, 1999).

1 Putting boredom in its place

Most books on boredom take the philosophical slant. This is the case for Reinhard Kuhn's *The Demon of Noontide: Ennui in Western Literature* (Princeton: Princeton University Press, 1976), Sean Desmond Healy's *Boredom, Self, and Culture* (Rutherford, NJ: Fairleigh Dickinson University Press, 1984), Orrin Klapp's *Overload and Boredom: Essays on the Quality of Life in an Information Society* (New York: Greenwood Press, 1986), Patricia Meyer Spacks' *Boredom: The Literary History of a State of Mind* (Chicago: University of Chicago Press, 1995), Michael Raposa's book, Lars Svendsen's *A Philosophy of Boredom* and Elizabeth Goodstein's *Experience without Qualities: Boredom and Modernity* (Stanford: Stanford University Press, 2005). Kathleen Norris' *Acedia & Me: A Marriage, Monks, and a Writer's Life* (New York: Riverhead, 2008) covers much of the same ground, but with a more interesting and personal slant and, like Michael Raposa, with a much more religious flavour.

There are a large number of very intriguing books in French on the same topic, but these waver between depression (usually termed melancholy) and boredom: Madeleine Bouchez, *L'Ennui: de Sénèque à Moravia* (Paris: Bordas, 1973), Norbert Jonard, *L'Ennui dans la littérature européenne: des origines à l'aube du XXe siècle* (Paris: Honoré Champion Éditeur, 1998) and Georges Minois, *Histoire du mal de vivre:*

de la mélancolie à la dépression (Paris: Editions de la Martinière, 2003) are good representatives. Jennifer Radden, *The Nature of Melancholy: From Aristotle to Kristeva* (New York: Oxford University Press, 2000) is in the same convention. The Russian tradition, strong until the Revolution, is represented by Oblomov (Ivan Goncharov, *Oblomov*, trans. David Magarshack [Harmondsworth: Penguin, 1978]).

To understand boredom, infinity and time I'd start with something frivolous: the *Independent*'s survey of boredom ('The Boring List: 20 Titans of Tedium', 14 March 2008) is an amusing way to do this. Mihaly Csikszentmihalyi's comments on boredom and the loss of a sense of time are more weighty, influential and can be found in *Beyond Boredom and Anxiety: Experiencing Flow in Work and Play* (San Francisco: Jossey-Bass, 1975/2000). My discussion of the status of boredom as an emotion is based on Antonio Damasio's *The Feeling of What Happens: Body and Emotion and the Making of Consciousness* (San Diego: Harcourt Inc., 1999) and *Looking for Spinoza: Joy, Sorrow, and the Feeling Brain* (San Diego: Harcourt, 2003). Damasio, as you would expect, is very instructive on the nature of disgust as an emotion.

For what constitutes an emotion and what are the emotions, an introduction can be found in Robert C. Solomon's 'Back to Basics: On the Very Idea of the "Basic Emotions"' in *Not Passion's Slave: Emotions and Choice* (Oxford: Oxford University Press, 2003). Disgust and boredom are linked by Robert Plutchik in, for example, *Emotion: Theory, Research, and Experience* (Washington: Academic Press, 1980). A more philosophical take on disgust is offered by Winfried Menninghaus, *Disgust: Theory and History of a Strong Emotion* (Albany: University of New York Press, 2003). For the cognitive approach to emotion I'd read David Konstan's excellent *The Emotions of the Ancient Greeks: Studies in Aristotle and Classical Literature* (Toronto: University of Toronto Press, 2006) and Daniel Gross' *The Secret History of Emotion: from Aristotle's 'Rhetoric' to Modern Brain Science* (Chicago: University of Chicago

Press, 2006). Catherine Lutz's *Unnatural Emotions: Everyday Sentiments on a Micronesian Atoll and their Challenge to Western Theory* (Chicago: University of Chicago Press, 1988) illustrates how emotions are coloured by their cultures, while Paul Ekman (in works such as *Emotions in the Human Face*, 2nd edn, Cambridge: Cambridge University Press, 1982) tries to show how emotional expressions can be universal. This has made him something of a whipping boy for those who deny universality in emotional expression. William Ian Miller's *The Anatomy of Disgust* (Cambridge, Mass.: Harvard University Press, 1997) is very helpful on the social and literary significance of disgust.

Children and boredom is a topic that comes up often and relates closely to the status of boredom as an emotion. There is not much written about it. One exception is the essay, 'On Being Bored', in Adam Phillips' *On Kissing, Tickling, and Being Bored: Psycholanalytic Essays on the Undiscovered Life* (Cambridge, Mass.: Harvard University Press, 1993).

There is little by way of assistance in examining the way boredom is depicted in visual art. The nearest help comes from the extraordinary catalogue of the exhibition on melancholy that was held at the Louvre in 2005: Jean Clair (ed.), *Mélancolie: génie et folie en occident* (Paris: Réunion des musées nationaux/Gallimard, 2005). Matilde Battistini's *Symbols and Allegories in Art* (trans. Stephen Sartarelli, Los Angeles: J. Paul Getty Museum, 2005) is sometimes helpful. For a discussion of yawning there is Andrew and Gordon Gallup's 'Yawning as a Prodromal Sign of Vaso-vagal Reaction', *Evolutionary Psychology*, 5 (2007), p. 92. The link between time and ADHD (and thus children) is discussed in Katya Rubia's article 'Impulsiveness as a Timing Disorder' in a special themed issue of *Philosophical Transactions of the Royal Society B*, July 2009. For novelty seeking there is also David H. Zald et al., 'Midbrain Dopamine Receptor Availability Is Inversely Associated with Novelty-Seeking Traits in Humans', *Journal of Neuroscience*, 28(53), 31 December 2008, 14372–14378.

2 Chronic boredom and the company it keeps

The Boredom Proneness Scale derives from R. Farmer and N.D. Sundberg, 'Boredom Proneness: The Development and Correlates of a New Scale,' *Journal of Personality Assessment*, 50 (1986), 4–17 (reprinted by permission of the publisher [Taylor & Francis Group, http://www.informaworld.com). Social scientists are particularly interested in chronic boredom. Two very helpful survey articles on boredom and the social sciences are by Anna Gosline: 'Bored?' *Scientific American*, 27 December 2007 and 'Bored to Death', *Scientific American*, 26 February 2007. The psychologist Stephen Vodanovich has written many useful articles on boredom of this type. I've cited his article written with Deborah Rupp: 'The Role of Boredom Proneness and Self-reported Anger and Aggression', *Journal of Social Behavior and Personality*, 12 (1997), 925–937. The dopamine articles are by G.A. Wiesbeck et al., 'Alcohol Dependence, Family History, and D2 Dopamine Receptor Function as Neuroendocrinologically Assessed with Apomorphine', *Drug and Alcohol Dependence*, 40 (1995), 49–53 and David H. Zald et al., 'Midbrain Dopamine Receptor Availability is Inversely Associated with Novelty-Seeking Traits in Humans'. Otto Fenichel's article is 'The Psychology of Boredom', in *Organization and Pathology of Thought: Selected Sources,* ed. David Rapaport (New York: Columbia University Press, 1963). Eric Dahlen's article is 'Boredom Proneness in Anger and Aggression: Effects of Impulsiveness and Sensation Seeking', *Personality and Individual Differences*, 37.8 (December 2004), 1615–1627.

It's understandable that people in business schools also worry about boredom. Their focus is the workplace and boredom there means lost profits. Cynthia Fisher's 'Boredom at Work: A Neglected Concept', *Human Relations*, 46 (1993), 395–417 aims to remedy the problem but offers as well a satisfying definition of the emotion. Educationalists worry over the emotion too and whether or not boredom impedes or improves children's progress in school. Teresa Belton and Esther Priyadharshini, 'Boredom and Schooling: A Cross-Disciplinary Exploration', *Cambridge*

Journal of Education, 37 (2007), 579–595, think it can help. Within indigenous communities boredom can lead to violence and substance abuse: Yasmine Musharbash, 'Boredom, Time, and Modernity: An Example from Aboriginal Australia', *American Anthropologist*, 109.2 (2007), 307–317. A good critique of the modern philosophical basis to much of the social scientists' approach to boredom is Ben Anderson, 'Time-stilled Space-slowed: How Boredom Matters', *Geoforum*, 35 (2004), 739–754.

Chronic boredom is often depicted in novels and in the cinema. It's seen here as destructive too, because of the often extreme means to which people will resort in order to escape from it. Reinhard Kuhn's *The Demon of Noontide* has much to say that is instructive on this topic. My discussion of chronic boredom in one of these novels (and its filmed version) was assisted by Fredric Jameson, that well known literary theorist from Duke University and his 'Historicism in *The Shining*', *Social Text*, 4 (1981), 114–125. Fictional characters who complain of boredom are often self-absorbed. For a social science take on this condition there is Hope M. Seib and Stephen J. Vodanovich, 'Cognitive Correlates of Boredom Proneness: The Role of Private Self-Consciousness and Absorption', *Journal of Psychology*, 132.6 (1998), 642–652. And some such fictional characters are prone to anger. A useful discussion of this link, from a psychological perspective, is Eric R. Dahlen et al., 'Boredom Proneness in Anger and Aggression: Effects of Impulsiveness and Sensation Seeking'. On traumatic brain injury (TBI) there is J. Danckert and A. Allman, 'Time Flies when you're having Fun: Temporal Estimation and the Experience of Boredom', *Brain and Cognition*, 59 (2005), 236–245.

On paranoia and boredom I've been helped by Mitchell J. von Gemmingen et al., 'Investigating the Relationships between Boredom Proneness, Paranoia, and Self-consciousness', *Personality and Individual Differences*, 34 (2003), 907–919 and Daniel and Jason Freeman, *Paranoia: The 21st-Century Fear* (Oxford: Oxford University Press, 2008). Joseph Ephraim Barmack's conclusions were published in the *Archives of Psychology*, No. 218, New York, 1937, the *Journal of Psychology*, 5 (1938), 125–133, and the *Journal of Experimental Psychology*, 25 (1939), 494–505. Boredom under the Raj is a fascinating topic – Jeffrey Auerbach's 'Imperial Boredom', *Common Knowledge* 11 (2005), 283–305, has much that is valuable to say on the matter. The best place to learn all about dromomania is Ian Hacking's *Mad Travellers: Reflections on the Reality of Transient Mental Illness* (London: Free Association Books, 1999). I've drawn the tale of Albert Dadas from this book. On apotemnophilia: Carl Elliott, 'A New Way to be Mad', *Atlantic Monthly*, December 2000, and Paul D. McGeoch et al., 'Apotemnophilia – the Neurological Basis of a "Psychological" Disorder', *Nature Precedings*, posted 18 March 2009.

3 Humans, animals and incarceration

Who knows what levels of self-consciousness are possessed by animals, especially those most like humans? Santino the chimp is discussed in the *New Scientist*, 14 March 2009: the quote from Mathias Osvath comes from that article. That very small children used to be denied self-consciousness, just like animals, may be relevant. Antonio Damasio (in his *The Feeling of What Happens*) cites with approval the contentions of Jerome Kagan (*The Second Year: The Emergence of Self-Awareness*, Cambridge, Mass.: Harvard University Press, 1981). They believe that self-consciousness comes by the eighteenth month.

The studies of animal boredom by Françoise Wemelsfelder are very insightful ('Animal Boredom: Is a Scientific Study of the Subjective Experiences of Animals Possible?' in *Advances in Animal Welfare Science 1984*, ed. M.W. Fox and L.S. Mickley [San Francisco: Martinus Nijhoffs 1985]); 'Boredom and Laboratory Animal Welfare', in *The Experimental Animal in Biomedical Research*, ed. B.E. Rollin, Boca Raton: CRC Press, 1990; and, most influentially, 'Animal Boredom: Understanding the Tedium of Their Lives', in *Mental Health and Well-being in Animals* (Oxford: Blackwell Publishing, 2005). Wemelsfelder maintains that she has observed the transition between boredom, agitation and anger, and depression in animals. The University of Colorado ethologist Marc Bekoff endorses her conclusions (*The Emotional Life of Animals,* New York: New World Library, 2007). Dr Wemelsfelder appears to have based her approach on that of Otto Fenichel ('The Psychology of Boredom', in *Organization and Pathology of Thought*) who follows in turn an earlier study by Theodor Lipps (which I have yet to see). Fenichel makes a distinction between normal and pathological boredom, and sees them as existing on the same experiential spectrum. William Deresiewicz's essay on loneliness is 'The End of Solitude', *The Chronicle of Higher Education,* 30 January 2009. More generally on the capacity of animals to experience social emotions there are the many books of Frans de Waal (such as: *Chimpanzee Politics: Power and Sex among Apes,* Baltimore, Md.: Johns Hopkins University Press, repr. 2007, or *The Age of Empathy: Nature's Lessons for a Kinder Society,* New York: Harmony Books, 2009).

The topic of mirror neurons and their contribution to the empathy debate (they were discovered in animals in the 1990s) is fascinating – De Waal can help. Confinement is one particular cause of boredom in animals. It's a problem for humans too, as Daniel Freeman and Jason Freeman (*Paranoia: The 21st-Century Fear*) and Stuart Grassian ('Psychopathological Effects of Solitary Confinement', *American Journal of Psychiatry,* 140 (1983), 1450–1454 and 'Psychiatric Effects of Solitary Confinement', *Journal of Law and Policy,* 22 (2006), 325–383) point out in their discussions of prisons. The material on Albert Speer is drawn from Albert Speer, *Spandau: The Secret Diaries,* trans. Richard and Clara Winston (New York: MacMillan Publishing, 1976). For the details of Meursault: Albert Camus, *The Outsider,* trans. Joseph Laredo (Harmondsworth: Penguin, 1982). Does incarceration affect brain mapping? Norman Doidge has a useful discussion of how environment can remap brains in his *The Brain that Changes Itself: Stories of Personal Triumph from the Frontiers of Brain Science* (New York: Vintage, 2007). Prison literature is a vast genre. It probably begins with Plato's *Apology*. Surprisingly, boredom is not an unvarying feature of this genre.

J.M. Barbalet's speculation on the difference between depression and boredom is to be found in 'Boredom and Social Meaning', *British Journal of Sociology*, 50 (1999), 631–646. The confusion between loneliness and boredom within the Warlpiri culture is provided by Yasmine Musharbash, 'Boredom, Time and Modernity: An Example from Aboriginal Australia,' *American Anthropologist*, 109.2 (2007), 307–317.

4 The disease that wasteth at noonday

This translation (and that for Cassian) derives from Siegfried Wenzel, *The Sin of Sloth: 'Acedia' in Medieval Thought and Literature* (Chapel Hill: University of North Carolina Press, 2003). I have adapted his version in places.

Elizabeth Goodstein (*Experience without Qualities: Boredom and Modernity*) is the most satisfying, compendious and acute of all of the writers who focus on the recent history of existential boredom. The single most inspiring book on this tradition, however, is one devoted to melancholia: it is Raymond Klibansky, Erwin Panofsky and Franz Saxl, *Saturn and Melancholy Studies in the History of Natural Philosophy, Religion and Art* (London: Nelson, 1964). Jennifer Radden's *The Nature of Melancholy*, also offers a wonderful survey of the nature of melancholia and how acedia can be seen within this. You can look at the tradition from a medical point of view as well, as did Stanley W. Jackson in his *Melancholia, and Depression: From Hippocratic Times to Modern Times* (New Haven: Yale University Press, 1986).

Klibansky et al. discuss acedia (Evagrius and John Cassian) as well as the Renaissance tradition that is associated with Albrecht Dürer and Lucas Cranach the Elder. Evagrius has recently been translated by

Robert E. Sinkewicz, *Evagrius of Pontus: The Greek Ascetic Corpus* (New York and Oxford: Oxford University Press, 2003). Siegfried Wenzel, *The Sin of Sloth*, also clarifies the meanings of acedia and provides texts of the authors I have discussed, although he does not believe that the real identification of acedia can be made. Kathleen Norris' *Acedia & Me: A Marriage, Monks, and a Writer's Life* (New York: Riverhead, 2008) offers both a moving and a fascinating personal view of acedia. I have discussed acedia and also the ancient traditions relating to boredom and nausea (and suicide) in *Melancholy, Love, and Time: Boundaries of the Self in Ancient Literature* (Ann Arbor: University of Michigan Press, 2004). Two recent books on the seven deadly sins are Solomon Schimmel, *The Seven Deadly Sins: Jewish, Christian, and Classical Reflections on Human Psychology* (New York: Oxford University Press, 1997) and Wendy Wasserstein, *Sloth* (New York: Oxford University Press, 2005).

Nausea and nausea are habitually linked with the emotion of boredom, especially in French criticism (I've already mentioned the surveys by Bouchez by 1973, Jonard 1998 and Minois 2003). But what they mean is something closer to existential boredom. The quotations from *Nausea* are taken from Jean-Paul Sartre, *Nausea*, intro. Richard Howard, trans. Lloyd Alexander (New York: New Directions Books, 2007). Annie Cohen-Solal's engrossing biography, *Sartre: A Life* (trans. Anna Cancogni, ed. Norman MacAfee [New York: Pantheon Books, 1987]) is the best help of all on nausea. The translation for Seneca is my own. There is considerable discussion of the interrelation of boredom and suicide in Al Alvarez' *The Savage God: A Study of Suicide* (London: Weidenfeld & Nicolson, 1971). I don't believe a word of it. Boredom, through its link with depression, can easily be conflated with madness. Consider how the titles of the following two books mix depression and madness: William Styron, *Darkness Visible: A Memoir of Madness* (New York: Random House, 1990) and Kay Redfield Jamison's *An Unquiet Mind: Memoirs of Moods and Madness* (London: Picador, 1996).

5 Does boredom have a history?

Most recent commentators in English insist that boredom is the invention either of the era of the European Enlightenment or of the Romantic period: so Lars Svendsen (*A Philosophy of Boredom*), Sean Desmond Healy (*Boredom, Self, and Culture*), Patricia Meyer Spacks (*Boredom*), Elizabeth Goodstein (*Experience without Qualities*), and Yasmine Musharbash ('Boredom, Time, and Modernity'). Constructionism, more generally, has lately come in for criticism: Paul Boghossian's *Fear of Knowledge: Against Relativism and Constructivism* (New York: Oxford University Press, 2006) is a famous example. Probably the best of the essentialists, however, are not philosophers like Boghossian, but scientists – the most stimulating are neurobiologists such as Antonio Damasio or sociobiologists such as the entomologist E.O. Wilson (*Sociobiology: The New Synthesis* [Cambridge, Mass.: Harvard University Press, 2000]) or primatologists such as Frans de Waal. (Criticism of this group best comes from Richard Lewontin [*Not in Our Genes: Biology, Ideology and Human Nature* (New York: Pantheon Books, 1984)] and Stephen Jay Gould [with Lewontin] 'The Spandrels of San Marco and the Panglossion Paradigm: A Critique of the Adaptationist Programme', *Proceedings of the Royal Society of London*, Series B 1161 (1979), 581–598].)

The French studies of boredom – such as that of Didier Nordon (mentioned below) – are not as insistent on boredom's being an invention of the Enlightenment. Maybe this is because of the link that the French make between boredom or ennui and depression. Depression, they seem to feel, has been with us over the *longue durée*.

There are lots of terms for boredom other than boredom. I've provided a limited survey of some of these and of their use in ancient Greece and Rome in my *Melancholy, Love, and Time*. Anne Szulmajster-Celnikier surveys the terms and expressions for boredom in approximately fifty languages in her 'À travers les langues' in Didier Nordon (ed.), *L'Ennui: féconde mélancolie* (Paris: Editions Autrement, 1998).

Very few of these were invented in the seventeenth or eighteenth centuries. Arthur Kleinman's *Patients and Healers in the Context of Culture: An Exploration of the Borderland between Anthropology, Medicine, and Psychiatry* (Berkeley: University of California Press, 1981) is very insightful in explaining how emotions are registered differently in different cultures (focusing especially on China). Nostalgia is not another term for boredom, but, sometimes, an approximate conceptual equivalent. Some useful discussions of nostalgia are Svetlana Boym's *The Future of Nostalgia* (New York: Basic Books, 2001), Fred Davis' *Yearning for Yesterday: A Sociology of Nostalgia* (New York: Free Press, 1979), Linda Austin's *Nostalgia in Transition: 1780–1917* (Charelottesville: University of Virginia Press, 2007), and David Vine's *Island of Shame: The Secret History of the US Military Base on Diego Garcia* (Princeton: Princeton University Press, 2009: p. 149ff. 'Dying of Sagren'). There is the old classic on the Golden Age and related ideas by Arthur O. Lovejoy and George Boas, *Primitivism and Related Ideas in Antiquity* (Baltimore: Johns Hopkins University Press, repr. 1997).

I might not agree with all of it, but I am full of admiration for Yasmine Musharbash's 'Boredom, Time, and Modernity'. I am looking forward to reading her *Yuendumu Everyday: Contemporary Life in Remote Aboriginal Australia* (Canberra: Aboriginal Studies Press, 2009). H.D Eastwell's article, 'Australian Aborigines', *Transcultural Psychiatric Research Review*, 19 (1982), 221–247, may be old now, but it is still very clear and to the point.

6 The long march back to boredom

Where is boredom? You can find out more about the insula in Antonio Damasio's *The Feeling of What Happens* or in *Looking for Spinoza* as well as in his 'The Somatic Marker Hypothesis and the Possible Functions of the Prefrontal Cortex', *Philosophical Transactions of the Royal Society of London*, Series B (Biological Sciences), 351 (1996), 1413–1420.

Antonio Damasio developed the theory relating to the function of the insula a decade ago. This was termed the 'somatic marker hypothesis'. It suggests that rational thinking cannot be separated from feelings and emotions, which is usually said to be an updated version of the thinking of the nineteenth-century American psychologist and philosopher William James: a very helpful overview of this topic is provided by Sandra Blakeslee, 'A Small Part of the Brain, and its Profound Effects', *New York Times*, 6 February 2007. I was also assisted by A.D. (Bud) Craig, 'How Do You Feel – Now? The anterior insula and human awareness', *Nature Reviews/Neuroscience*, 10 (2009), 59–70. Frank Stanish has directed me to Andrew J. Calder et al., 'Disgust sensitivity predicts the insula and alladial response to pictures of disgusting foods', *European Journal of Neuroscience*, 25 (2007), and Xiaoyun Liang et al., 'Effective connectivity between amygdala and orbitofrontal cortex differentiates the perception of facial expressions', *Social Neuroscience*, 4.2 (2009). If the April 2009 report for the UK's National Institute for Economic and Social Research has its way ('How to Pay for the Crisis or Macroeconomic Implications of Pension Reform' by Ray Barrell, Ian Hurst and Simon Kirby: http://www.niesr.ac.uk/pdf/EWLfin.pdf) then the insula is going to be given a thorough working out during the next few decades. As for the cures for the stressed insula: the most accessible discussion of neural plasticity and its curative implications for boredom (by implication) and depression is contained in Norman Doidge's *The Brain that Changes Itself.*

For a really stimulating, non-medical discussion of the role of free time, leisure and play and how they may combat boredom it is still very hard to beat Sebastian de Grazia's *Of Time, Work, and Leisure* (New York: Vintage Books, repr. 1994). For exercise (and boredom) there is Sue Halpern's *Can't Remember What I Forgot: The Good News from the Front Lines of Memory Research* (New York: Harmony Books, 2008). Does music help to cure boredom? The *Guardian* story on the musical Belfast elephants was by James Randerson and appeared on

17 November 2008. Charles Snowdon's and David Teie's work on music and chimps was published in *Biology Letters* in September 2009. Some of the curative agents for dementia are outlined in Benedict Carey's article on ageing which was published in the *New York Times*, 21 May 2009. Adorno's 'Free Time' can be found in *The Culture Industry: Selected Essays on Mass Culture*, ed. with an intro. J.M. Bernstein (London and New York: Routledge, 1991). The clip from Kraepelin is on page 2 of Lewis Wolpert's moving *Malignant Sadness: The Anatomy of Depression* (London: Faber and Faber, 2001).

Christopher Lane's discussion of how shyness has been over-medicalized is *Shyness: How a Normal Behaviour Became a Sickness* (New Haven and London: Yale University Press, 2008). The discussion of sadness is by Allan V. Horowitz and Jerome C. Wakefield, *The Loss of Sadness: How Psychiatry Transformed Normal Sorrow into Depressive Disorder* (New York: Oxford University Press, 2007). There is a brief update of this theme in Jessica Marshall's 'Woes be gone', *New Scientist*, 14 January 2009, 36–39. I attempted a somewhat similar argument, but applied to the ancient world, in my *Melancholy, Love, and Time*. There is a useful review article on the opposite of sadness, happiness, by the egregious Sue Halpern, 'Are You Happy?' *New York Review of Books*, 3 April 2008.

Acknowledgements

Heather McCallum commissioned this book and got it started. Rachael Lonsdale finished it off. Working with Heather and Rachael has been an extraordinarily enjoyable and stimulating experience. There is not a paragraph nor even a sentence in this book whose structure and logic Rachael has not *patiently* improved. My daughter, Kathleen Toohey, found for me most of the artwork and illustrations in this volume and helped me to understand them. Lars Svendsen responded readily to a number of requests. So too – as always – did my old friend Peter Dale. And so did some of the people with whom I am fortunate to work or associate: Mark Golden, Hanne Sigismund Nielsen (for the Latin inscriptions from Beneventum and Pompeii), Haijo Westra (for many conversations and for the loan of books), and Ian Worthington (for suggesting I contact Yale with this book). Much of the project was sketched out while I was on sabbatical leave from the University of Calgary during the winter term of 2008. My reading has been assisted by a grant from the Social Sciences and Humanities Research Council of Canada (SSHRC). The book reached its conclusion thanks to an Izaak Walton Killam Resident Fellowship at the University of Calgary during the winter term of 2009. Two of my graduate students, Nicole Wilson and Jason McClure, pitched in. My gratitude, as ever, to my family: Phyl, Kate, Matt and Lindsay.

Index